To Dwi...

Best Wishes

How to Measure
Human Resources Management

How to Measure Human Resources Management

Jac Fitz-enz, Ph.D.

Saratoga Institute

McGraw-Hill Book Company

New York   St. Louis   San Francisco   Auckland   Bogotá   Hamburg
London   Madrid   Mexico   Montreal   New Delhi
Panama   Paris   São Paulo   Singapore   Sydney   Tokyo   Toronto

This book is printed on recycled, acid-free paper containing a minimum of 50% recycled de-inked fiber.

Library of Congress Cataloging in Publication Data
Fitz-enz, Jac
  How to measure human resources management.

  Includes index.
  1. Personnel management.   2. Personnel departments.
I. Title.
HF5549.F555   1984   658.3   83-19965
ISBN 0-07-021131-0

            13 14 15 DODO 9 8 7 6 5 4 3 2

ISBN 0-07-021131-0

The editors for this book were William Newton, Bonnie Binkert,
and Dorick Byard; the designer was Mark E. Safran; and the production supervisor was Teresa F. Leaden. It was set in Melior by
Datagraphics, Inc.

Printed and bound by R. R. Donnelley & Sons Company.

To My Parents, Kathryn and Art
Thank You

Contents

Preface

This is a book about success in organizations. To be more precise, it is about how to be more successful in running a human resources department in a modern organization. Success is built on your ability to do your job, the wisdom to spend your time on the issues which are important, and the skill to communicate your results. I believe that the management of people is the most important task of any organization. If that is true, then it follows that the professionals who are directly charged with building the systems to attract, pay, counsel, and develop employees ought to be esteemed members of the management team. In too many companies that is not the case. This book is designed to help you win a spot on the first team.

THE LANGUAGE OF BUSINESS

If the language of business is dollars, then the alphabet is numbers. All organizations, whether profit or not-for-profit, depend on their ability to get the best possible return on dollars invested. Even some governmental agencies who thought they were immune from this basic law have found themselves severely cut back by an electorate which demands service in return for their tax dollars. Managers of human resources functions have long labored under the burden of lean staffs and tight budgets. Part of the reason for this has been their inability to communicate with management in the language of business.

THE APPROACH

My method is experiential and very practical. There is little reference to theory and even less to statistics. Although we will deal with numbers throughout the book, the mathematics are very basic. The four functions of arithmetic will take care of 99 percent of the applications discussed. The design is the result of 12 years of running personnel and training functions. The last six of those years were spent developing and refining a total system concept for quantifying human resources management. Since 1978, I have conducted public workshops on this subject. The ideas, formulas, and reports you will find in this book are a result of my concept, enriched with the valuable suggestions of the hundreds of human resources practitioners, consultants, and college professors who have attended the workshops.

I believe this book represents the most comprehensive text on the subject available today. I do not expect that you will drop everything you already know and adopt this system. I hope that initially you will find the philosophical basis sound and that it might be a source of inspiration for you to rethink what your purpose is in the organization. Once you are secure in the knowledge of what you want to construct, this book is like a big tool box. It can help you build the structure necessary to achieve your goal. I expect you will use the tools selectively, as this book is not intended as a panacea. Everyone's environment is somewhat unique. I cannot tell you what you need. I can only give you the tool box and explain where and how to use each tool. You must decide which of the formulas and reports are useful in your situation.

THE STYLE AND PLAN

My style is familiar and direct. I use the editorial "we" very seldom. I want to talk with you just as though we were in the same room together. I want to discuss common human resources issues with you and give you some ideas on how to deal with them. I have divided the book into an introductory section, four applications sections, and a short concluding section on the payoffs and rewards to be found in this approach.

Section A provides a short history of the human resources profession. It lays out the issues of measurability and talks about some of the fundamental questions of human resources management. The section concludes with a chapter on how to generate quantitative measures for the human resources department. Sections B through E provide detailed explanations with examples of how to measure the four main human resources functions: planning and staffing, compensation and benefits, employee relations, and training and development. Section F provides examples of organizational and individual payoffs, which are the result of the quantitative approach to human resources management.

My plan was to write a book which would be useful to people working at many levels within a human resources department. In addition, I wanted to provide a new perspective for the senior- and graduate-level college student of human resources management.

ACKNOWLEDGEMENTS

My first and most sincere thank you must go to the people who over the years told me that we cannot or should not quantify the work of the personnel and training departments. They challenged me to keep working on the conceptual and mechanical problems. By now, most people agree that we should be able to objectively evaluate our work. But those early doubters were a great inspiration. I want to thank Toronto consultant Tom Handley, Ida Meyers of Tektronix, Walt Whitt of American Express, Barb Schoneberger of Internorth, Ginny McMinn of Rustoleum, Harry Garner of Northern Telecom, Lon Boncyk of Computervision, Susan Bailey of Best Products, and Bert Mastrov and Bob Lopresto of Korn-Ferry for supporting my work and recommending it to others. In particular, I would like to thank Richard Israel for telling me repeatedly that I had a valuable concept and not to be discouraged by critics. Deep appreciation goes to the staff at the American Society for Personnel Administration: Marsha, Debbie, Shirley, Tom, Jeff, and retired executive director, Len Brice for supporting my workshop as we all worked to make it as effective as possible. I also want to thank the people I worked with from 1976 to 1982 at Four-Phase Systems' industrial relations department. They took my ideas, added value, and turned them into an excellent system. Special support came from Kathryn Hards, Pat Morton, Sharon Bue, Barbara Kuenzel, and Bob Coon.

Along the way many others contributed also and I regret that I cannot mention all their names. One of the most important people in this endeavor is Esther Hunt. Esther did research, typed the manuscript, and offered whatever support was needed when it was needed. Finally, I would like to thank my wife, Ellen Kieffer, who put aside much of our social life for the past year so that I could spend the time it takes to write a book. She encouraged me to do it and provided loving advice all along the way. Without her it would have gotten done, but it would not have been as good a product.

Jac Fitz-enz

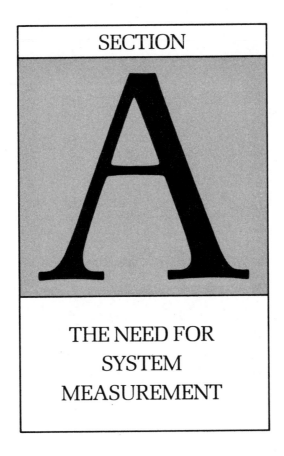

SECTION

A

THE NEED FOR
SYSTEM
MEASUREMENT

Prologue: How We Got Here

STAGE ONE: A SLOW START

In the late 1800s the industrial revolution overwhelmed the United States. In the space of two decades it replaced small business for all time as the center of commercial activity. With the growth of giant steel, railroad, petroleum, and electrical companies came the creation of staff departments, one of which was personnel. The personnel department usually was formed to meet the need to recruit thousands of people to work the machines of the new age. It was staffed of necessity by employees from line functions, and there was no formal education for personnel work. Once on the job there was little opportunity for training since there was no one truly qualified by years of experience to do such training. Hence early personnel work was pretty much trial and error. Since the value systems of nineteenth-century industrialists focused on new ways to engineer and manufacture, the people function and the worker in general were not highly valued. Employees were treated like production parts and personnel like inventory clerks. Although most organizations are now more enlightened in their treatment of workers, this attitude has not totally disappeared. I remember vividly how the president of a company I worked for described the personnel department to a visiting VIP. He opened the door to the department, stepped in, and said to his guest, "this is where they keep employee records." The man nodded and they turned and left.

In time, personnel departments came to be staffed by individuals who could be released from the "more important" functions of manufacturing, sales, and finance. In effect, the department often became the dumping ground for the organization's casualties. When well-liked employees began to have performance problems, a decision might be made to place them in personnel rather than fire them. After all, the feeling was, "they can't hurt anybody there."

Admittedly, there were some individuals who willingly chose personnel as a career field. They had enough interest to find ways to acquire the rudimentary skills necessary to do an adequate job. Nevertheless, this was more the exception than the rule in the early days. Although it began to change after World War II, there are still a few organizations which persist in using personnel as a holding tank for the organization's mistakes. So long as this is the case, the department will never have a contributing function.

STAGE TWO: THE SERVICE MODEL

Between the two world wars, the personnel function began to develop. By the late 1940s it had become more than an offshoot of payroll. Besides being an employment service, it took the first step toward creating sophisticated compensation systems. Training blossomed during the postwar boom, when millions of veterans were returning and looking for jobs in both traditional and new industries. The training technologies which had been developed in the service began to find their way into industry, and personnel fell heir to much of that new capability. Labor relations, which had matured before most other functions, continued to be important as unions again flexed the muscles which they had voluntarily left unused during the war.

Two traits characterized the changing personnel department. First, it was largely a reactive service; that is, there was not a great deal of forward planning. While the organization might develop elaborate short- and long-term business plans, little effort was made to carry that over to the full range of personnel subjects. Some work was done to generate gross numbers of employees needed to meet the business plan. Still, most companies did not begin to think of manning tables and succession planning with its implications for training until well into the second half of the century. Personnel was often not privy to the highest management councils. Hence, it had little choice except to be reactive.

The second characteristic of the postwar period was a continuation of the attitude that labor was an adversary and not a partner of management. This supported the view that employees were an element of cost and not an asset. It was only during the 1960s that this view began to change. Given these attitudes and values, personnel work was directed toward a maintenance mode. The idea was that no news from personnel was good news.

STAGE THREE: OPPORTUNITY

The third and current stage owes its birth to government intervention into private business. As much as any other force, the federal government changed the way organizations related to and managed their employees. It is a rather consistent phenomenon that when any individual, group, or institution achieves a power advantage he, she, or it tends to guard that edge with great vigor. Change occurs when a greater power comes along. In this case the power was the federal courts and Congress.

The 1960s and 1970s saw the passage of the Civil Rights Act, ERISA, ADEA, and OSHA. Each act found a different point of entry into the organization. In an effort to deal with these new realities, organizations placed the responsibility with the personnel group and staffed to meet the intrusion. The problem had created a need for competency. No longer could an organization afford to load personnel with its misfits. At last, young people saw an opportunity for interesting work and perhaps even satisfying careers. As they entered the personnel function and began to show results, management came to see possibilities they had never before imagined could exist there. No other single force did as much good for the professionalism of personnel as did Uncle Sam.

Three other factors have also played roles in the recent development of the personnel profession. The first was the evolution of the work force itself. A profound social change had begun to take place in the United States. The baby boom of the late 1940s and early 1950s threw a large number of young people into the labor market around 1970. Not only were they young, but they were also better educated than their parents. More importantly, their values were different. No longer content with just a job, they demanded meaning and satisfaction from their labors. Compounding this, many oppressed people began to find their voices. Women and minorities, with the support of zealous federal agencies, pressured for a piece of the action and demanded that organizations provide a wide range of welfare benefits and social activities in addition to simply employment.

Another important factor was the rapid postwar growth of organizations themselves. Both in size and scope of markets, the industrial concerns of the 1970s dwarfed those of the 1930s. Some companies now do as much business in the Orient or the Near East alone as their predecessors used to do in the entire world. This has brought new requirements for specialists in areas such as expatriate compensation and intercultural training. Questions of centralization or decentralization of multibillion dollar corporations are being delegated to personnel for study and for a role in implementation.

Finally, most recently, the slowdown in the growth of industrial productivity has become one of the nation's most pressing problems. Many personnel departments are becoming involved by designing new pay plans, conducting training and organizational development interventions, and setting up quality of work life programs. It is here, within the productivity dilemma, that personnel has been handed its greatest opportunity. Some departments have taken advantage of it. In doing so they have moved from the reactive and peripheral mode of stage two toward a more involved and strategic position.

In conclusion, it is clear that personnel has undergone a three-step evolution from being a tolerated minor function to finding itself on the threshold of becoming one of the major factors in the management of large, complex organizations.

You Can't Measure What We Do

THE SUBJECTIVITY MYTH

A mythology has developed around personnel work. It has to do with the nature and purpose of the work, and more importantly, it deals with the outcomes or results of the labor. The fundamental belief is that personnel is something of a complex and mysterious art. Allegedly, the true and full value of the work can only be judged by those who perform it. Even then, the appraisal is bounded by subjective criteria. Many of the faithful believe that, like virtue, personnel work is its own reward. Terms used to describe results are satisfied, quick, better, interesting, good, important, creative, and other similar nonspecific terms.

There is an ingrained notion that business-type measures cannot be applied to this function. There are even some who believe that personnel is not a business activity, even though it exists in, and is funded by, a business organization. They see organizations basically as suppliers of jobs. The goals of productivity and profitability are seen as something to be promoted only if they can be achieved in conjunction with employee satisfaction.

Whether the subjective position is valid or not is a key question to be sure. However, just the fact that it exists and that many personnel people support it is a major problem. It sets personnel apart from the rest of the organization. While their peers in other departments are focusing on income, assets and liabilities, sales, costs, and profits, personnel workers are talking about feelings. It is a communication gap of the most basic type. Line managers quickly learn that personnel has neither understanding nor interest in financial matters. Therefore, when there are meetings to review business performance or to plan future business moves, personnel is not invited to sit in. As a result, programs and projects are set in motion and personnel is told what their role will be after the fact. At that point it is too late for the function to make any meaningful input to the program. All it can do is carry out its predetermined role. Most personnel managers resent this second-hand treatment, yet it is inevitable given the apparent lack of common interests and common language.

REASONS WHY NOT

There are a number of reasons which account for the lack of quantification in personnel. Probably the most prevalent is that personnel people simply do not know how to objectively measure their activity. There are many routes into personnel management. Few, if any, offer training in quantitative methods. Many senior people in personnel today have worked their way up from clerical or recruiter positions. Since the chances are better than 9 out of 10 that their predecessors did not have quantitative measurement systems, it follows that contemporary managers are never exposed to a measurement methodology. Therefore, it is not surprising that most of them rely on subjectivity.

The newer generation has sometimes had an opportunity to study personnel administration in college. Unfortunately, statistical courses are not a part of many personnel administration curricula. Even when they are, they tend to be either financial or behavioral science methods. Statistical procedures have seldom been adapted to the creation of input-output ratios for measuring the function's results. The reason for this is simple: most academics have never applied themselves to the problem. There are some schools which have developed a few measures, but they have done such a good job of not talking about it that almost no one knows it. Likewise, the seminar market has not taken up the question. Promoters of public workshops have seldom offered sections on quantitative techniques. As of the end of 1982 only two public workshops were available on this subject. In summary, for someone who wants to start a measurement system in their department there is very little help available.

The second reason behind the subjectivity myth is the values conflict. Some believe that objectivity is simply inappropriate for personnel. In their eyes, personnel is a function devoted to stimulating and supporting human development, and they see no reason to evaluate outcomes in other than humanitarian terms. This one-sided attitude is prevalent in many occupations. Some teachers believe their sole mission is to transfer information from their brain into the notebooks of the students. They take no responsibility for teaching students to think, evaluate, or form values. Some architects believe their job is to create a container within which some kind of activity can be efficiently carried out. They overlook the fact that human beings interact with the space and can be depressed or stimulated by it. These perspectives ignore the holistic philosophies which emerged in the 1960s.

For those whose value systems conflict with the notion of measuring personnel, there is little hope for change. They see only a small part of the raison d'etre of personnel. Until they expand their outlook to include supporting the purpose of the organization which employs their subjects, there will be no change.

Another very common reason why most personnel departments are not measured is that many managers of personnel and training fear measurement. Once when I was making a presentation to the management staff of a Fortune 500 company I was stopped by the training manager, who said that he collected some of the data that I was discussing. I congratulated him and asked him how he used it. He said, "I don't." When I asked why, he answered, "because I don't want anybody to know how I'm doing."

I have never fully understood that attitude. Perhaps it is born from a fear of knowing. My assumption is always that people are doing a good job. I agree that if you are doing a poor job the last thing you should do is publish a report on it. But in most cases people are doing at least an adequate job, and they usually improve over time. So fear should not be a factor. This brings us to the fourth and last reason for the subjectivity myth.

Top management has bought the myth of subjectivity. Perhaps because there was little interest in the personnel function, the early captains of industry simply never asked the question. As time progressed, the tradition of nonmeasurability went unchallenged. Few chief executive officers (CEOs) have taken more than a cursory tour in the personnel department during their careers. Personnel is often only a quick stop on the way to the executive suite. Just about the time that they began to get a feel for what might be accomplished, they are off to their next developmental assignment. In order to get into the guts of any department it takes time and a belief that there will be a payoff for one's effort. A 12-month tour in the personnel department of a major corporation is hardly enough time to understand each of the sections. Most young executives, knowing that the assignment will be brief, look for a quick project with a lot of visibility. They tend toward programs in compensation or training rather than a major, fundamental improvement project which would touch all facets of the department. Soon they move onward and upward, and inevitably the myth is perpetuated.

If the current condition is to change, top management will probably have to take some responsibility and act. There are two ways they can promote a change. First, they can demand that an objective reporting system be created by the existing personnel department. In order for that to happen, they may have to focus on the function and review the level of resources committed to it. This could include training in measurement methods for the incumbents, or it might mean bringing in a consultant. Second, they could hire a person who knows how to put a system in place. That will be difficult, but not impossible. There are companies who have such systems in various states of development. Personnel managers who have run these systems are usually upwardly mobile and willing to move. The payoff for creating a fully functional quantitative system will become obvious as we proceed.

DRUCKER ON MEASUREMENT

Peter Drucker, one of foremost experts on management today, speaks about the issue of measurement in several of his writings. He makes two basic assertions. First, he states that few factors are as important to the performance of the organization as measurement. Second, he laments the fact that measurement is the weakest area in management today. W. Edwards Deming, a pioneer in statistical methods for quality control, points out that in Japan great emphasis is placed on statistics for business managers. It was partly the application of the statistical techniques taught by Deming which turned postwar Japan from a manufacturer of cheap imitations to a worldwide leader in quality products.

It seems inevitable, given the demands that will be made on personnel in the future, that measurement must become a part of the function. During the 1930s when Joseph Tiffin and Ernest McCormick led the industrial psychology department at Purdue, they had a motto: "If you can't measure it, forget it." The underlying idea was that if you wanted to do meaningful work in industry you had better design it in such a way that you could do cost-benefit analysis of the effort and the result. If you could not find an observable outcome which could be objectively evaluated, it probably wasn't a worthwhile project in the first place.

Somehow over the past 40 years that presumption has been lost by personnel. With the advent of the human relations movement after World War II, quantification became the province of the industrial engineer. Over the next three decades personnel drifted slowly and somewhat aimlessly through subjective waters. At last, there are scattered signs of a rebirth of interest in a modified version of the Purdue ideal.

The Pros versus the Cons

SUCCESS IN ORGANIZATIONS

Success in organizations is dependent on three abilities. First, you have to be able to do your job. Just meeting the standards is not enough; you must excel. I assume that you can do that and I am not going to tell you anything about how to do your job better. Second, you must excel in the right areas. That is, you need to focus your attention and energy on the issues that make a difference. This is a failing of many staff departments because they look at their mission inside-out instead of outside-in. Inside-out refers to the "me-first" approach. The inside-outers look at what they want to do first and then try to bring the organization around to their values. Inevitably this fails. The outside-inners look at their client organization and ask, "What do they need from me?" Then, they structure themselves to provide that service or product. This does not mean that they give up their convictions, but they simply recognize that there are other valid viewpoints and that staff departments are in existence to support the mission of the organization and not vice versa. All of us on the staff side would do well to keep this pragmatic principle in mind.

Finally, success depends on your ability to take measures of your performance and use them persuasively to obtain the resources you need. This is the ability we will focus on in this book. It is a two-phase skill. First, you need to be able to develop data about your performance in a form which is meaningful to your audiences. I say audiences because there are several. One is your department. You must communicate with the people you work with in ways which inform, compliment, criticize, stimulate, and reward them, because without them you will achieve nothing. Another audience is the various departments and managers you interact with to service or to obtain cooperation to perform your responsibilities. Obviously, informative and persuasive communication is critical in these relationships. The other audience is senior management. This includes everyone in the system above your level. That is where the power is, and if you want to tap it you must be able to inform and persuade the people who hold it.

This leads us to the second phase. There is no getting away from it; we are all salespeople. Although few people realize it, more than 50 percent of our communications are persuasive in nature. Research has proved that many of the seemingly unimportant comments we make are really attempts to turn others to our way of thinking or to make them act according to our wishes. Test it if you like. Stand at the edge of any conversation and listen to how much of it is claims and assertions and how much is pure information offered with no desire to persuade.

To summarize, if you want to be successful over the long term, you have to do three things well: you have to excel at your job; you have to perform in areas which positively impact the mission and purpose of the larger organization; and last, but also very important, you have to be able to use information about your performance which proves to the organization that you are doing an excellent job and that you should be given whatever it is you are seeking.

THE NAME OF THE GAME

Business is and always has been a numbers game. With the advancements in information processing technology, today's executive has access to a range of data which is nearly infinite in its depth and breadth. There is almost nothing that a computer can't process at incomprehensible speed. The price-performance curve on computers is declining so rapidly that before the 1980s are over desktop microprocessors will offer most of the capability that today's multimillion dollar corporate computer does.

Computers today are churning out numbers on sales volume, accounts receivable and payable, production efficiency, market penetration, and hundreds of other subjects including projections for the future. The numbers tell management how much something costs, how many units are being produced and sold, and how long the lead time is for delivery of parts or products. They are not only descriptive, they are also predictive. In short, they drive the business.

Periodically, businesses report on their progress by issuing press releases and filing required public reports with the government. Probably the most widely read report is the annual public relations product entitled the annual report. This four-color high-priced glossy document is generally divided into two parts. The first is a narrative section which is devoted to a message from the CEO and a picture story covering company products, customers, and general activities. This is the place where you find the CEO's "people are our most important resource" statement. The second section is filled with financial data, numbers, and explanations of accounting treatments.

If you want to know how well the company is doing, you don't spend much time in the front of the report. Bankers and securities analysts, people who make their living by their ability to diagnose the health of a company, turn immediately to the back of the book. They want to see the numbers, because words are too imprecise. The government and the accounting profession have combined to establish what are called generally accepted accounting principles. Analysts, using these principles for clarification, can read the financial statement in an annual report and feel comfortable that they are learning the true condition of an enterprise.

There is no escaping numbers. Without them the line departments would have little idea of their performance, and there would be no way to attract investors. Also it would be impossible to report to the stockholders. Top management cannot run a modern large corporation if it does not have numbers to work with. This being the case, how is personnel to exist in the organization? Surveys have shown that, although they knew the number of employees in the company,

> A majority of major corporation personnel directors couldn't state the dollar volume of sales for their company, didn't know the profit level, and had little idea of the rate of return.[1]

These issues are all part of the daily life of the line manager. The conclusion is obvious: if we want to be effective communicators in business, we have to build rapport with our audiences. The most direct way to do that is by identifying with their values and using their language to communicate with them.

SELLING THE STAFF

The first time you introduce the idea of developing a measurement system to your staff, you will probably be greeted with a mixture of reactions ranging from apathy to rebellion. The first objection is usually, "I don't need anything else to do. I am already overworked and underpaid." The next is, "what are you going to do with the data? Will it be used to compare one person to another so you can fire the poorest performer?" That comment is followed by, "I don't see any value in doing it," "I don't think it can be done," and finally, "what's in it for me?"

All of these are reasonable reactions. They reflect the fact that this is a new concept for many personnel workers. People are fearful of change unless they see a good reason for it. The introduction of a measurement system is such a radical departure from the norm that it is bound to create fear, suspicion, and opposition. It is nothing to be concerned about since there are very plausible answers to these objections.

The staff has to be convinced on four points: first, that there is a valid business reason for doing it; second, that it can be done; third, that it won't mean a lot of extra work; and last, that there is definitely something in it for them. We will discuss these points one at a time.

Number one: there is a valid reason for doing it. This department is part of a business organization, whether you are a profit or a not-for-profit corporation. Personnel is not so unique that it can be run under its own separate philosophy, with a somewhat introverted set of objectives and a method of management that does not fit in with the larger organization which it supposedly serves. Personnel is part of an organization, and derives its support from it. We operate according to its philosophy and serve its objectives. We use its compensation system and its review and discipline policies. Like most staff departments, our work infiltrates the whole organization, and that body in turn absorbs us and sustains us. It is truly a symbiotic relationship. Therefore, since the larger organization runs quantitative methods, in order to be in sync with it we need to adopt its methodology for interfacing and reporting results.

The second objection is the belief that measurement cannot be done. The next chapter will provide an in-depth treatment of the manner in which the total personnel function can be broken down into manageable and measurable pieces. A review of the preceding discussion of the myth of subjectivity may also be helpful in formulating an answer. The point is that it is already being done in small and large departments in other organizations. There are some techniques to be learned, but a measurement system is much less complicated than a salary structure or a recruitment program. Once in place, it does not need constant updating to remain competitive or to cope with short-term changes in the job market.

The third objection is difficult to disprove until the system is actually in place. On first glance, it does look like a lot of extra work. Data must be collected from who knows where, a collection method must be designed, and a reporting format must be created. And that is only the beginning. Once it's all ready to go, some poor fool is going to have to make it happen. All of this is true, but like any task there is an easy way and a hard way to do it.

The critical element of a measurement system is the collection of data. Once you have the data, the reporting system is relatively simple. The secret to easy data collection is to make it part of the job that generates it. That is, workers are responsible for the development of their own raw data. If your system is automated, the computer may do the job for you. If you are manually collecting the data, workers simply maintain a log of the activities you want to measure. You may design standard logs or you may let them create and maintain their own. It doesn't matter so long as the data is complete, accurate, and turned in on time.

However, some people will say that logs get in the way and slow down the work. With practice, that need not be the case. When an activity such as an interview, a counseling session, a training class, a new-hire record, an agency invoice approval, or a termination is completed, it takes only seconds to record that in a properly designed log. At the end of a reporting period—say, a month—employees total their data and forward it to someone who fills in a master report form. For 6 years I managed a personnel department which ran a system that measured 30 to 40 activities. Most of our data was collected and recorded manually. We calculated that it took less than 5 percent of our total work time to maintain the system. That was not 5 percent work time *added* to the day: it was part of doing the job and therefore soon became invisible. Every group, no matter how busy it is, has more than 5 percent wasted time lying around. The value of having the data far outweighs the labor.

This leaves us with the final question, "what is in it for me?" People have a right to know what the payoff will be for them. They will be the ones who will do most of the work. Fortunately, there are several rewards for those who make the system work. As you read through the book, look for payoffs from measurement. Discuss them with your staff. When you reach Section F, The Payoffs, see if you have found as many as I list there. I'll bet you will have found many more.

THE SEMANTICS OF MEASUREMENT

Before we go any further, it might be prudent to define some terms and discuss some fundamental issues of measurement. The objective will be to foster clarity and to avoid semantic debates. Humpty Dumpty pointed out to Alice the ambiguous nature of words. "When I use a word," Humpty said, "it means just what I choose it to mean—nothing more nor less." Words are by their nature only neutral symbols. People give them meaning, sometimes in a rather haphazard fashion. This practice is particularly true in the case of the words efficient, productive, and effective. In everyday conversation these terms are often used interchangeably, and even the dictionary definitions are similar. However, the terms connote slightly different outcomes.

Efficient versus Productive versus Effective

Productive is defined as "producing readily or abundantly." Synonyms for productive are profitable, fertile, and fruitful. The definition of *efficient* is "competent or adequate in performance or operation," which is similar to productive but implies something less potent. Capable and causative are synonyms for efficient. So, while both productive and efficient are positive terms, productive infers something beyond mere competence. The third word, *effective,* takes the notion of productivity and adds a notion of expectation or desirability. It is, as Peter Drucker puts it, "doing the right thing."[2] Another definition of effectiveness is, "having the desired effect or producing the expected result." With this as a foundation, we will use efficient to mean simply an acceptable level of throughput or performance. Productive means efficiency directed at activities which have real value. An example might be a case where a person performs a task very quickly and neatly and is therefore efficient. However, the task is one which adds nothing to the output of the department and cannot be described as a productive act. Drucker's definition of effectiveness as doing the right thing, in an efficient manner, will serve our purpose.

Direct and Indirect

Two other words will be used to describe different types of measures: direct and indirect. A *direct measure* is one which refers to cost. It could be the cost of hiring, the cost of a benefit plan, or the cost of a training program. An *indirect measure* is one which does not deal with cost. It could be a measure of time, quantity, or quality. In many cases indirect measures can be converted to direct measures through the introduction of some conversion variable. An example would be converting the indirect measure of the time it takes to interview into the direct measure of the cost of interviewing. If we know that on average it takes our interviewers 1½ hours to interview a managerial-level job applicant and we know the hourly pay rate of our interviewers, it is a simple matter to multiply that pay rate by 1½ to obtain the cost of the interview. This is a very simplistic example. Obviously, there are other costs involved in an interview. Depending on how precise you want to be, you can add in overhead and benefit costs, or any other cost item which is appropriate, to obtain the total cost of the interview. The point is that indirect measures have a value in and of themselves and they also supply part of the data needed to develop a direct measure.

Whole and Partial

A subset of both direct and indirect measures is the difference between whole and partial measures. In this case, the terms are self-descriptive. *Whole measures* describe the total issue. For example the cost per hire which includes every expense item would be a whole measure. However, if you just want to calculate the cost per hire using a particular source, such as agencies, you would be working toward a *partial measure* of hiring costs. In that case you would probably take all other costs as givens and would want to know only how much agency fees amounted to per hire.

Whole measures are informative on a broad basis. If you want to learn where you are spending most of your time or money you will dissect the whole measure into two or more categories or parts. By breaking down total cost by source, department, job level, race, sex, occupation, or other categories you can find out where the problems lie or where the opportunities for improvements are.

PRECISION LEVELS

Any time the subject of measuring personnel work comes up it is interesting to listen to the wide range of perceptions held by our colleagues. Some show no concern for the complexity of the task and seem willing to jump into the middle of it without a moment's pause. Others fret over a multitude of minor, solvable issues, apparently looking for reasons why they cannot or should not attempt it.

In the latter cases, invariably someone brings up the point of accuracy or precision. Their point usually is that it is difficult, if not impossible, to accurately measure personnel activities. They point out their lack of control over factors such as inflation and labor market conditions. They are right, but similar conditions prevail throughout the organization. The marketing department does not have control over the product marketplace and the finance department does not control the cost of money. Yet both of them are able to quantitatively evaluate much of their work. Everyone knows that certain factors are not controllable. In fact, if we were willing to admit it, there are probably more issues out of control than in control within any organization. The task of management is to reduce the uncontrolled and install as much order as possible.

Management does not require accuracy at the .05 level of significance. In research, precision is obviously critical. In pharmaceuticals or medicine, extreme care must be taken with procedures and measurement. Results are often required to be statistically valid beyond the .001 level. That is measurement with a capital M. But, it is not what is required in operational measurement. We are not in a laboratory, we are operating in the field with all the problems inherent in field research and experimentation. Accuracy is necessary, but precision is naturally limited by internal and external conditions.

In order to play the numbers game it is not necessary to introduce heavy statistics. Performance measurement of the type we are advocating can be handled with the four basic arithmetic functions. Knowledge of statistical procedures is helpful for designing a measurement system which will have the most validity possible. Nevertheless, an acceptable job can be done by someone who simply has experience in the function; common sense; and the ability to add, subtract, multiply, and divide.

On one occasion a professor from a midwestern university complained that my method, while effective, was too simple. My reply was, "if you think these formulas are too simple of a way to express the conditions they observe, how would you evaluate $E = mc^2$?" He replied, "I don't know anything about chemistry."

There is a truism about measurement: anything which can be seen and described can be measured. Any object, issue, act, process, or activity which can be described by observable variables is subject to measurement. The phenomenon can be evaluated in terms of cost, time, quantity, or quality. (The technique for accomplishing this will be described in Chapter 4.) The only real issue in applying measurement to the personnel function is: what is worth measuring?

REPORTING

Contrary to the individual in Chapter 1 who did not want anyone to know how he was doing, most people who go through the effort of collecting data and measuring their activities want to report their accomplishments to management. Report design is an art form which is not fully appreciated. Many people believe that it is simply a matter of arranging data on paper or a film medium and presenting it to some audience. These people seldom have much success in moving their audience in any desired direction.

Reports have two purposes: they both inform and persuade. Whether or not they achieve either purpose depends on the skill of the reporter as much as on the data presented. Reports should tell your story and simultaneously convince your audience that you are a professional manager who is in control of your function. In order to do this, your audience will have to take the time to read or view your report. To grab and hold their attention you have to speak to them in forms which they comprehend and appreciate. Chapter 4 will cover reports in greater depth.

Remember, you can do a great job, but if you cannot tell your story effectively you will never get credit for your accomplishments.

CHAPTER 3

Starting Over

PERSONNEL AS A SYSTEM

Quantitative measurement of the human resources function is such a radical change for many people that it is almost like starting over. It requires not only a new way of doing the job, but a new way of thinking about it.

An idea which has been very useful in helping us grasp the complexity of large, modern organizations is *systems theory.* A simple definition of a *system* is an assemblage of parts put together in a somewhat orderly fashion to form a complex whole. Each system is usually composed of smaller systems, called *subsystems,* and is also part of a larger system. The notion of the world as a mosaic of interrelated systems quickly becomes apparent. Systems thinking is not a twentieth-century concept. It is not the by-product of modern scientific technology. John Donne pointed it out over 350 years ago when he said,

> No man is an island, entire of itself; every man is a piece of the continent, a part of the main.[3]

In their simplest form, systems take something from the environment, called an input; change it through a process; and then release the changed item back into the environment as an output. More complex systems have established goals or objectives toward which they process the input, plus a feedback mechanism to keep them on track. Complex systems not only receive inputs and make outputs to the external world, but also exchange inputs and outputs among internal subsystems. That is, the outputs of one subsystem become the inputs of an-

21

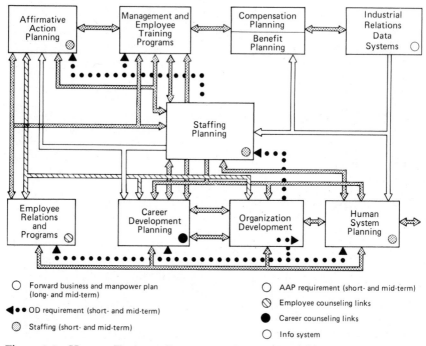

Figure 3.1   Human Resource Department System Model

other. There is an inherent interrelationship and interdependency between the parts of any large system. This is perhaps the most critical issue which human resources staffs have to learn if they are to survive and prosper.

The HR (human resources) department is a system. Its primary subsystems are staffing, planning, employee relations, compensation and benefits, training, and development. Even casual consideration of the HR department in action shows that there is constant, necessary interaction among the subsystems. For example, inputs to staffing in the form of applicants are processed and output to the external organization as new hires and to the HR department as input to the records. Later those new hires will be input to the orientation and compensation functions. Still later they will impact training and perhaps employee relations. Each time employees are touched by one function within the HR department they are transformed somewhat, and those transformed individuals then become input to another function. Therefore, the quality of work in one section affects the process for the next section in the system.

Figure 3.1 is a conceptualization of an HR department as a system.

It shows the connections between the various subsystems, or sections. Once this system is set in motion, the intensity of interaction is easy to imagine.

Personnel work is often practiced in a fragmented fashion. Staffing groups focus on the job of providing qualified new hires. Compensation strives to maintain equity in pay and benefits for all employees. Training teaches people new knowledge and skills. Each group seems oblivious to the work of the others, and there is seldom any evidence of collective activities. While this is inefficient for optimum organizational performance, it is often a sign of a much more dangerous illness in the departmental organism. The combination of a parochial view of the human resources function and the need to survive in a sometimes hostile environment prevents some human resources people from supporting their colleagues.

Thus, the HR department is often the subject of both just and unjust criticism. Sometimes the critic will complain to someone from one function about what is perceived as poor performance in another function. For example, an employee may comment to a trainer that the staffing function is very slow in filling one particular critical position. Rather than point out to the complainer that that particular skill might be very hard to find in today's market, the trainer agrees that some recruiters do not seem to be very creative with sourcing. If this type of nonsupport becomes a pattern of behavior among the human resources staff, the employees outside of the HR department begin to believe that the department must be as bad or worse than they suppose it is because even the people within it do not defend it. As a result, personnel's reputation suffers, the organization's confidence in the function declines, resources are withheld, and in difficult times the staff is reduced.

In order to establish and maintain a healthy, high-performing HR department, the function must be operated as a mutually supportive system. It cannot ignore the intrinsic interrelationships among subsystems, and cannot be effective on a fragmented basis. There must be an acceptance of the principle of unity. Every individual, whether professional or clerical, must understand Donne's premise that the loss of any individual diminishes all of us. Human resources is one department, one unit, inextricably bound together. Success and failure are collective, not individual, phenomena.

PHILOSOPHY-VALUES-BEHAVIOR

The humanistic psychologist Abraham Maslow formulated a motivation theory which states that the most fundamental human needs are survival and safety. We want to feel secure both physically and psychologically. Organizations generally provide physical security for their employees. To the extent that the organization is financially healthy, most employees can feel free from capricious action on the part of management. Psychological needs are not as easily fulfilled. The foundations of psychological security are rooted in a philosophy and a set of values to which an individual can subscribe. A philosophy and a value system are the antecedents of behavior. Once a person accepts a philosophy of life and a purpose and blends it with a compatible value system, the question of acceptable behavior is easily resolved.

Behavior is ultimately determined by our perception of ourselves as individuals and of our purpose and role within the setting in which we operate. In order for an employee to know how to behave there must be organizational philosophies and values. Whether or not these types of issues are discussed in the work place the employee looks for them, wants them, and finally creates them from whatever is available.

It is much more effective for an organization to take the time to formulate and disseminate a philosophy than it is for the employee to have to search for and perhaps misperceive an organizational belief system. If an organizational philosophy already exists, it is easy to draw up an appropriate departmental statement. If a philosophy is not apparent, the task is still not too difficult. An example of the types of statements which could express an HR department's philosophy is as follows:

- Human resources exists in an organization because it provides a necessary function at a competitive cost.
- Human resources' mission is to enhance the productivity and effectiveness of the organization as it relates to both people–people and people–system interfaces.
- Human resources should drive the organization's management in regard to people issues.
- Human resources is a professional function, staffed by people dedicated to the development of employees in ways which are satisfying to the individual and beneficial to the organization.

Once the philosophy has been formed, the next step is to work out a set of values which fit the philosophy. Values are social customs or ideals which a group regards as positive or negative. The Boy Scout oath —a scout is courteous, clean, kind, brave, reverent, and cheerful—is an example of group values. A value system plays the role of a link between philosophy and behavior. Within an organization it helps an employee connect somewhat abstract philosophical statements with rather specific related behavior. Organizational values might include such concepts as the following:

- Allowance for risk taking and making mistakes
- Clear expectations
- Contribution-oriented
- Flexibility
- Fun
- A growth versus maintenance perspective
- High standards
- Honesty and trustworthiness
- Loyalty
- Mutual support
- Optimistic and constructive
- Personal growth
- Personal pride
- Personal responsibility
- Proactive/initiating
- Respect for all

All that is required to round out the system is to develop a list of acceptable, expected behaviors. Since behavior is somewhat role determined, it is necessary to describe behaviors for employees at different levels. Managers have certain expected role-based tasks, and employees

Organization values	Attendant behaviors
Allowance for risk taking and mistakes	Managers: delegate and support Nonmanagers: give careful thought to ratio. potential impact of actions Everyone: refrain from open criticism of others' mistakes
High standards	Managers: set formal levels of acceptable preformance Nonmanagers: set challenging personal goals
Loyalty	Everyone: speak well of colleagues at all times to all people
Proactive/initiating	Managers: set out and find what the market needs Everyone: look for opportunities; ask for new responsibilities
Personal responsibility	Everyone: don't blame others; if you don't like it, negotiate a change or fix it

have other role-based tasks. Yet some behaviors pertain to management and employees, regardless of rank. To deal with role and rank issues, behavioral statements may be expressed in three categories: managerial, nonmanagerial, and everyone.

Since values and behaviors are linked so closely, I repeat some of the values statements with examples of attendant behaviors on page 25.

This exercise in establishing a departmental philosophy, developing organizational values which everyone can accept, and describing attendant behaviors has been very useful to a number of HR departments who were having staff morale problems. If this process is carried out in a participative manner, at least through the supervisory level, the participants feel a sense of ownership and commitment to the product. Everyone is clear about what is appropriate. If they choose not to subscribe to the values of the company, they are free to look for an organization which is more compatible with their style. As a result, no matter whether people buy it or not, the most fundamental principles of operation have been promulgated and no one can claim not to know what is expected and acceptable.

SERVICE OR SUPPORT?

Part of the starting-over process is the issue of self-perception. In order for a new way of thinking and acting to become permanent it must be consistent with the individual's view of self. For many years human resources has been described as a service function. Service is defined as "performing labor for the benefit of others." The inferior attitude implied in this definition seems to have infected many people both in management and in the HR department. When someone has an inferiority complex, they communicate it verbally and nonverbally to those around them. Perhaps the most dysfunctional result is that employees lose respect for and will not follow the advice of the human resources staff members who exude this inferior self-image. It is no wonder that under such conditions one hears the now familiar lament, "I don't get no respect around here."

I suggest we drop the word "service" as a descriptor for the HR department and instead use the term "support." Support is defined in slightly more positive tones; there is a feeling of necessity and of something closer to equality. Synonyms for support are assist, encourage, confirm, and defend. There is not a great deal of difference between service and support, but again there is a more positive tone to the latter. Over the past few years I have discussed this comparison with many people. Most had never thought about it, but as we talked they all agreed that they had a more positive feeling about the term support. It is a subtle difference, but I believe it is an important one. After all, most campaigns—whether in sports, war, or love—are won through a series of small yet significant gains, which start with a positive self-perception that is communicated to others.

An amusing method for testing your staff's self-perceptions is the automobile game. This parlor game can be played at a staff meeting both for fun and to uncover hidden morale issues. Very simply, ask the people this question. "If the human resources department were an automobile, what part do you think you would be?"

When such an absurd metaphor is used, people seldom feel threatened about answering it truthfully. We have found that people at all levels of the HR department freely express themselves when asked this question. Using a metaphor as their reference point they are not bound to think of themselves in their formal organizational roles. They become very creative in their search for just the right part that expresses how they feel about themselves as human beings and the functional role they play in the department.

In a way, this game is a projective test. People project themselves into a mental picture of a car in a way which is compatible with their self-image. Both positive and negative analogies are expressed. Some claim to be the steering wheel which directs the function, the gasoline which makes it go, or the hood ornament which symbolizes its beauty. Others talk about being the bumpers that are constantly run into, the trunk that is always at the end in the dark, the turn signals which flash first one way and then the other, or the exhaust pipe which emits only the by-product of energy—hot gas.

Some people choose images which reflect only their self-image. Others select ones that relate only to their job, and not to themselves. A few innocent questions bring out a great deal of information about self and job perception. This can be used to improve individual and departmental morale. The game's value is that not only does it develop good information, but it is a lot of fun and a break in the often too-serious business of work.

Another party that must be considered in our reexamination process is the client: management. There are a number of studies which have shown that the HR department and management do not see eye to eye on what the HR department's role is, should be, or could be.

White and Wolfe[4] carried out a study through the American Society for Personnel Administration (ASPA) in which they queried over 800 personnel and line managers on current and desired practices in personnel administration. They concluded that the line welcomed relatively high and increasing involvement by personnel in providing support services and advice. At the same time, they noted lack of mutual agreement as to what functions are appropriate to personnel. White and Wolfe cited other studies where this gap of understanding also occurred. It was suggested that the personnel director "should shape, and not be shaped by, circumstances."

A survey conducted by the Opinion Research Corporation[5] asked a number of questions of both top and operating management and human resources management regarding present and desired functioning of the HR department. Basically, top and operating management said that it expected the HR department to make contributions, particularly in training and development, employee communications, career and succession planning, and compensation. Human resources managers generally agreed, but their priorities were not in the same order. When asked about the future, top and operating management emphasized more attention to management development, increasing productivity, and a better trained and more professional staff.

In summary, it is clear that most managers want the HR department to be an active and vital contributor. It is also obvious that the HR department has an opportunity to at least partially define its role. How this is handled will dictate whether or not the HR department takes advantage of the opportunities offered in stage three.

THE BOTTOM LINE

Measurement has a role to play in the system we have just discussed. It does more than simply evaluate performance. A measurement system provides a frame of reference which helps management carry out several important responsibilities.

1. Focuses the Staff on Important Issues.   Organizations are complex, intense places. There are many forces competing for attention and energy. If a measurement program is designed as a supporting subsystem, it will differentiate tasks for the staff according to higher and lesser priorities. If cost reduction is a major issue in an employment group, that helps recruiters decide how to source applicants. They can select sources which may take more time but are cheaper. For trainers, it tells them to bring a program in-house rather than send people to a public seminar. Thus, the cost per trainee hour of instruction is reduced. Fundamentally, the staff learns that cost, time, quality, and quantity are trade-offs around which decisions and actions take place.

2. Clarifies Expectations.   A measurement system is not inert nor reactive—it is directive and clarifying. Once objectives are set for cost, time, quality, and quantity the staff knows what is expected of them. Standards of performance and acceptable levels of deviation from those standards are known. If objectives are set to reduce hire costs, third-step grievances, and training time, or to increase record processing efficiency and turnaround time on application forwarding, the staff knows what is acceptable performance.

3. Involves, Motivates, and Fosters Creativity. My experience has been that once a measurement system is in place the staff begins to compete to meet or exceed the objectives. Once the system is fully functioning, people bring forth new and important issues that can be measured, along with ingenious ways of doing it.

Since the human resources staff occupies slots at different levels from management, their view is correspondingly different. Therefore, they find items that can or should be dealt with which the director of human resources might never see. Everyone enjoys bringing something up to the boss that has not been thought of before. Once measurement objectives are promulgated, people naturally focus on the variables therein and as a result often find something truly valuable which has been overlooked.

4. Brings Human Resources Closer to Line Departments. One of the most consistent complaints of line management is that the human resources staff does not seem to be interested in the important issues of the organization, namely ROI. Cawsey sums up an often heard criticism about the traditional personnel function as follows:

> As a service function, the human resources department doesn't have a clear, direct link to the generation of profit—the bottom line. Sales vice-presidents or sales managers can track sales which link directly to profits. Production vice-presidents or managers can track production cost and volume, both of which relate directly to profits. If you ask the traditional human resources manager how things are going, there is little he can say other than, "Things seem okay; people are smiling."[6]

You know there is much more that could be said. When the HR department stops reporting feelings and begins to report efficiency and productivity data it will be perceived as a mainline function and not as a nice-to-do activity.

Designing Your Measurement System

FINDING MEASURABLE ACTIVITIES

In Chapter 1 I discussed the subjectivity myth which still persists with some of our colleagues. I noted that one of the reasons for this myth was the fact that many people have never been exposed to measurement methods. As a result they simply do not know how to go about building a measurement system. There is no reason for this ignorance to continue. Any one of three different methods can be used to find measurable events, and each method is equally valid. Some are more complex than others, but all are easy to understand and execute.

The first and most common way of developing a list of just about anything is the tried and proved brainstorming approach. Most everyone is familiar with this. A group of people are given a question or a problem to solve. In this case the question is, "Among all the activity occurring within this human resources function, what can we quantitatively measure?" The participants are given time to deliberate and then are asked for their answers. All suggestions are taken and recorded without any judgments being rendered until all the ideas have been exhausted. It is normal to list these on a chart pad or blackboard so that all can see them. Often the sight of one measure will trigger the idea of another measure not previously thought of. After all the ideas are on the board or pad, the group goes back through the list and selects those which they all agree are worth working on. This method is relatively quick, and it gives everyone a chance to contribute. However, it usually does not produce as many measures as the other methods.

A second, less common but more powerful approach is the nominal group technique (NGT). This method is similar to brainstorming in some respects. They both start with the same question and in both cases the participants have time to deliberate. In NGT the participants generate their ideas in writing. Then, in round-robin fashion each member of the group offers one idea in a short phrase which is recorded on a flip chart or board. After all ideas are recorded each is checked with the group for clarification and evaluation. The final step is individual voting on the items by priority, with the group decision being mathematically derived through rank-ordering or rating. The nominal group technique is a highly developed form of brainstorming. Research has shown that if the task is idea generation, NGT produces more and better quality ideas than the standard brainstorming session.

The third method of measures generation is the matrix approach. When my management staff and I began to design our measurement system we were able to develop only about 15 measures. We designed our system around that first batch of measures and ran it for about a year. Then we believed that we could handle more so we went to brainstorming. Try as we might we simply recycled about 15 to 20 measures. Then I recalled someone saying, "You can't find new ways of doing things by looking at them harder in the old way."

With that in mind we radically changed our approach. Instead of looking for specific things to measure, we said, "why don't we see if we can more fully understand what is going on in our department?" Starting there, we began to describe our work environment variable by variable. Taking one function at a time we asked ourselves, "if we were to walk into Department X tomorrow what would we see?" We began to list every visible thing and every process that was going on. After we had listed everything we could think of, we then put them on a matrix and cross-matched each variable with every other variable. This literally exploded the number of measurable activities.

In all of the above cases the objective is to find what in statistics are called *dependent variables.* A dependent variable is, in this case, an activity which is subject to quantifiable measurement and whose value or cost can be increased or decreased through the manipulation of other factors called *independent variables.* For example, if we want to cut the cost of training we could start measuring the cost per trainee hour of our instruction. Cost per trainee hour (CTH) is the dependent variable. In order to calculate that value we have to know all the cost items which go into the training. This might include material expense, instructor salary, participants' salaries, travel expense, and room and refreshment cost. We also need to know how many people were trained and how many hours each was trained in order to calculate total trainee hours. All of these items are independent variables. By changing any of the independent variables we affect the dependent variable. We will see an example of this in the next section.

In conclusion, the point is that measurement development is a two-step process. First, by using the matrix method we generate a list of dependent variables which we choose to measure. Then, for each dependent variable we must decide which independent variables need to go into the calculation. Once we have those we can construct a formula which becomes part of our system of measures. In many trials I have always found that the matrix method is superior to brainstorming or nominal group techniques for generating a larger number of measures whose quality is at least equal to those resulting from other approaches.

HOW TO MATRIX

The easiest way to describe the matrix method is by example. Let us say that we want to generate a large list of measures for the staffing function. The first question is, "if you walked into the staffing department, what would you see?" You would see people: the staffing manager, supervisors, recruiters, clerks, applicants, new hires, and client managers (those looking to fill jobs in their group). You would see things: applications and resumes, requisitions, furniture and equipment, office spaces, bills for ads and agency fees, travel vouchers, referral bonus checks, and job postings. You would see processes going on: interviews, application screening, telephone calls, counseling, selection and rejection, record processing, and filing. All of these variables are subject to at least one of the four dimensions of measurement. Each can be analyzed according to its cost, the time it takes to do it, its quantity or volume or frequency of occurrence, or its quality. At this stage it is not important to know which of these attributes will apply. All you want to do here is fully describe the environment of the staffing department. Once you have a full description, you will probably be amazed at the size of the list. There should be at least two or three dozen variables. If you are meticulous in your observations, you may find many more than that. You may think that the list is too large, but don't feel overwhelmed. The list can be reduced without loss of value.

Go back over the list and decide if there are variables on it which you are not interested in measuring. You will undoubtedly find items which may be combined with others into a larger classification or which are not important to look at right now. An example of the first type would be furniture and equipment, office spaces, heat, and light. These are normally grouped into an account titled overhead. By substi-

tuting overhead for a half-dozen other variables you not only shorten
the list but also have a variable which has some meaning. Each of the
specific simple variables deals with an issue which, in and of itself,
probably does not have much importance. However, when combined
with the others to make an overhead category, the variable becomes
complex and may be worth looking at. In the case of the second type
of exclusion, some items just have no value now or perhaps ever. You
may decide that the number or duration of telephone calls is not an
interesting measure. You could decide to include the telephone bill in
with general overhead, or you might decide to just ignore it except as
an item within the total department budget or expenditure. Filing is
another example of a variable which probably has little value. If you
ask yourself what is really important for you to pay attention to and for
management to know about the staffing function, the key variables will
become apparent. Once you have reduced the list to a manageable
number you are ready for the next step.

Figure 4.1 is a sample of the matrix form which you will use to lay
out your variables. Referring to your final list of useful variables, begin
to write them in on the lines coming off the left axis of the grid. Starting

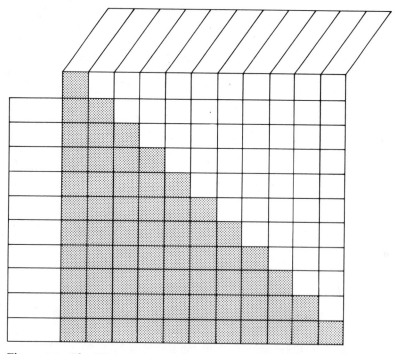

Figure 4.1 The Measurement Matrix

at the top left corner, put one variable on each line going vertically down the left side of the grid. Start with cost, then time, and proceed in any order you want thereafter. Do not worry that these variables are all opposite blackened spaces on the grid. Since you will probably have a list which exceeds twenty variables, I suggest that you do this on a blackboard or on a couple of chart-pad sheets taped together. The grid should be large enough to have a line both vertically and horizontally for each variable on your final list. When you have finished going down the grid turn your attention to the spaces across the top. Again, beginning at the top left corner of the grid, write in one variable per line going left to right across the top of the grid. These must be in the same order as the one you used vertically. For example, you started your vertical list with cost and time and let's say you followed with recruiters, clerks, applicants, and hires. Then, your horizontal list must start with cost and time and follow the same sequence (recruiters, clerks, applicants, hires) from left to right across the top of the grid. The end product should be a grid which has the same list of variables running down the side as it does across the top. You will then have created a matrix of useful variables.

The next procedure will be to begin to match a vertical with a horizontal variable line by line. The grid has 121 cells or squares in it. Each cell is a combination of two variables. One comes from the list on the side and one comes from the list on the top. The first thing you would notice if none of the cells were blackened is that the top left corner cell is a combination of the same variable from the top and from the side. This is really not a combination, is it? It is redundant. If we were to create a dependent variable called cost per cost it would be nonsense. Hence, redundant cells are useless. If you go to the next line down and across you will find that time and time fill the second cell down and the second cell in to create another redundancy. Following that pattern you would see that there is a line of redundant cells which run from the top left corner to the bottom right corner. All of them are useless and therefore have been blackened. But, what about all the other cells to the left of that line? They are not redundant, but they are duplicates of cells on the right side of the line.

To test them, select two variables, let's say clerks and requisitions. They are the fourth and seventh variables, respectively, on the side and on the top. Follow the clerk line horizontally from the left side until you reach the cell under requisitions. That is four down and seven across. You have a clerk/requisition combination to look at to see if there is a useful dependent measure there, for example, the number of requisitions processed per clerk. Now go back to the left side to the requisition line and follow it horizontally to the right until you are under the clerk column. You find that it is just the reverse position from the preceding case. It is seven cells down and four across, and it is the same combination in reverse, requisitions/clerk. Since your mind can quickly flip the equation back and forth from C/R to R/C it is unnecessary to bother with duplicate cells. For that reason the cells in the lower left half of the grid have been eliminated.

While focusing only on the top right side of the grid you will still have every combination possible among the ten variables. In a 11 X 11 grid you have 121 cells. Through the procedure just described we have eliminated 66 cells without any loss of possibilities. What you have left is 55 possible combinations of variables which might be useful dependent measures. The next step is to begin matching them.

Probably the easiest way is to start again at the top left corner and proceed horizontally along the line to the right, checking each cell as you go for a useful combination. So, the first cell now is the combination of cost (across) and time (down). Is cost over time (C/T) or time over cost (T/C) a worthwhile measure? At first glance most people would say yes. However, the answer is no. The reason is that there is no context of what kind of cost or time we would measure. Cost per hire or time to hire might make sense, but cost versus time alone is too amorphous. Hence, this cell is worthless. You have quickly learned that all 55 cells will not yield useful measures, but don't worry. I promise you that the product of your labor here will result in more dependent measures than you will want to track. So, let us continue.

The next combination to the right on the cost line is cost and recruiters. Is there a combination of cost and recruiter which makes sense to you? Perhaps you could use the cost of maintaining a recruiter in some formula. Would it be useful to have the cost per hour of a recruiter to factor into a formula such as cost per hire? If you want to know the average cost of hiring new employees one of the cost components is labor cost. So you would need the fully burdened hourly rate of a recruiter multipled by the average amount of time that you find your recruiters spend generating each hire. Recruiter cost becomes useful as an independent measure in this example. If you recall the discussion of personnel as a system you may remember we said that the department is made up of subsystems which feed other subsystems to create the whole. This is a minute example of that point. Sometimes a variable or combination of variables serves as an independent variable and in other cases as a dependent variable. The complexity of the human resources function becomes apparent when you look at it on the variable level. It is this complexity which has frightened off many who have tried to measure the function. But, you see that there is nothing to fear. If you reduce the department to its elements, namely the variables, it becomes relatively easy to track the activity and discover the interactions. Someone once said, "You cannot eat a whole cow with one bite. But, if you cut it up and take your time, sooner or later you will have disposed of the whole animal."

Moving further to the right along the cost line we come to cost and clerk. Is this worthwhile? The same rule applies here as it did with the recruiter variable. Next stop to the right is applicants. How about cost to process an applicant? It is up to you since there is no rule of usefulness. If it helps you it is useful, and if it doesn't forget it and go on. At this stage in the development of quantitative measurement for human resources there are no generally accepted accounting principles. Choose what you will, and report whatever you like. The only rule that applies is be consistent in your methodology and selection of independent variables, which we will discuss further below.

Continuing to the right we come to hires. Probably the most basic measure in the business is cost per hire. If people measure anything they tend to measure the cost of hiring. The only cases I am aware of when this is not a useful measure is if a company is the major employer in town. In that case there is usually a large waiting list of people who want to work at the company. A sign on the fence or a simple help wanted ad almost always generates more candidates than the company needs. In these instances, the recruiting variable of hiring cost is virtually nothing.

The next cell in the matrix is requisitions. The question is what is the cost per requisition? How much does your company spend just processing requisitions? Do you care to know? Is it necessary to have this number as an independent variable in another formula? If the answer to all these is no, you can probably proceed to the next cell.

How about calculating the cost per interview? This measure may have value as part of a cost per hire measure. For every hire there are often many interviews. If you want a very precise total cost of hiring, then you would need to know the average cost per interview and the average number of interviews per hire.

The last two variables are used in many ways. You can look at the total amount spent on ads or agencies. You can run comparisons on a per hire basis. You need them as components in a total cost per hire formula. They can also be used in combination with time. You can compare the average cost and the average time to fill a job using ads versus agencies to make a business decision. You may trade off high cost for quick response if you have a critical job to fill. If there is no rush and you are after expense reduction you can give up the better time source for the better cost source (assuming they are different).

There you have it. We have run trials of cost against all other variables on the list. Some were found to be basic and probably necessary, others were highly discretionary. The choices are yours and the people with whom you work. Simply recycle now and start over on the time line. When you have finished this list of 11 variables and 55 potential measures, you will fully understand how to generate measures in any situation. The procedure is always the same: make a list of variables; matrix them on a grid; eliminate redundant and duplicate cells; match each variable against all other variables, one at a time; and then make decisions as to each combination's usefulness. You will always produce more variables than you need. The only question is, "which ones do I want to use now?"

CREATING FORMULAS

Now that you have created a number of dependent variables, there are a couple of tasks left to do. This is not the end, but rather it is the beginning. These measures can only be realized if the independent variables which comprise them are identified and put into a formula. If we use a complex measure like cost per hire (C/H) as an example, the process is quite easy to understand.

There are two basic components to this measure: cost and hires. The first thing to do is identify all the cost elements. There are advertising charges (AC), agency fees (AF), bonuses to employees for referrals (in some companies) (RB), recruiter and clerical time costs (ST), client time costs (the manager with the job opening) (MT), overhead (OH), possibly travel and relocation expenses (T&R), and miscellaneous costs. These symbols are shown below in equation form.

$$AC + AF + RB + ST + MT + OH + T\&R + Misc$$

After you are satisfied that you have accounted for all cost items draw a line under them and go to the hiring issue. This is simple. It is the number of people hired during the time period that the expenses were incurred. It is expressed as H below.

$$\frac{AC + AF + RB + ST + MT + OH + T\&R + Misc}{H}$$

This completes the ratio, but not the equation. To do that, add the dependent measure C/H in front.

$$C/H = \frac{AC + AF + RB + ST + MT + OH + T\&R + Misc}{H}$$

This gives you the total, or what is usually called the *whole direct measure.* It is whole because it includes all variables and accounts for all hires. It is direct because it can be directly related to costs of operating the organization. Direct measures are always identifiable by the fact that they are measuring some kind of cost. Indirect measures do not cover cost, but do describe some measure of time (which can be converted to cost), quantity, or quality. Indirect measures—such as the number of counseling sessions held, the number of records processed, or the number of trainee hours of instruction conducted—also have value in the attempt to understand and evaluate how effectively an HR department is operating.

While whole measures are very beneficial for the management of the department, they often are too simplistic for problem-identification or problem-solving purposes. In order to fully appreciate and be able to differentiate activity and results among groups it is necessary to subdivide the data. As an example, cost per hire numbers can be subdivided by source of hire, level of hires, occupational groups, departments or divisions, and time periods. As we discuss specific measures further, you will see examples of how this adds meaning to the numbers.

RESULTS ORIENTATION

The definition of a manager is one who gets things done through working with people. The focus is working with people to get *results*. Many people in staff jobs fall in love with the process. A description of their

Function	Staffing		
Activities	General recruitment	College recruitment	Transfers
Tasks/Processes	Write and place ads	Contact placement offices	Post jobs
	Contact agencies	Schedule campus interviews	Screen
	Promote employee referrals	Interview on campus	Counsel
	Schedule interviews	Invite to visit company	Interviews
	Interview	Etc.	Etc.
	Refer		
	Reject		
	Make offers		
		Impact on production and profits	
Results	Hires	Hires	Placements Counselings

Figure 4.2   Function Analysis—the Staffing Function

work might be something like, "does things with people." Their focus is on activity. As we conclude this discussion of the issues and problems in human resources work, I want to fix your attention on results.

As you go through the following sections you will study many functions, activities, tasks, and processes. You want to view them, not for themselves, but for their instrumental value. That is, how to deal with them so that you will achieve positive results in the basics of cost, time, quantity, and quality. One way to keep focused on results is to do a functional analysis on each of the major HR department functions. Figure 4.2 is a partial example of a functional analysis of staffing.

There are many tasks and processes to handle to achieve a hire. You will want to measure some of them to the degree that they can tell you how efficient your staff is with them. But, the variable which ultimately makes or breaks you is results. What did it cost? How much time did it take? How many hires did you accomplish? What was the quality of the hires? How did it impact organizational profitability? These are the things you need to pay attention to. When you can prove that you achieved positive results in key areas, you will have established yourself as a valued member of the management team.

WHY REPORTS ARE IMPORTANT

I will conclude this section with a few points about reports. You now know how to make formulas to measure your work, and you have been reminded to focus on results, not activities. The last issue is communication. You can do a marvelous job, but if you cannot communicate your many worthwhile achievements, no one will ever know what you have done. If you want recognition for your results, it is almost as important to be an effective report writer as it is to be an effective manager.

Report generation is often approached as though it were either a weak piece of fiction or a textbook. In the first case, there are a lot of unsubstantiated statements, loosely connected, leading to a conclusion that is all too apparent. In the latter instance, there is a massive dump of information, seemingly with no form or direction, which challenges the reader to find something, anything, of value in it.

Every report should have a purpose and an audience. If both of those are not clearly defined before the data is assembled and the format chosen, the chances for a meaningful document are lessened. Reports are not sterile descriptions of inorganic chemistry. They describe, or should describe, the activities of often large numbers of human beings who are utilizing resources to achieve predetermined objectives. As such, they deserve a spark of life and a hint of personality. They should be interesting as well as informative. Dull reports bore readers, and what's worse they don't get read.

A report cannot be a neutral document. It must say something that causes the reader to make a decision. Even basic monthly reports of operation cause the reader to do something because a problem is evident, or to do nothing because all seems well. Project and investigative reports usually evoke more activity than conditional reports. Whatever the type, the report writer should keep in mind that the report has a purpose.

The purpose of any communication is to either inform or persuade. Since reports are forms or media for communicating certain types of organizational information, they too should perform one of the two tasks. If a report is primarily informational it displays the following characteristics: clarity, conciseness, accuracy, and appropriateness. Whether you are using words or graphics, remember that this is not meant to be a mystery story. Ask someone who is not involved in the process being reported to read the report for clarity. If they, who know nothing about the subject, can understand what you are trying to say, the chances are good that your reader will understand also. If you use some type of chart or graph, remember that graphic formats have special attributes and certain limitations. Keep the graphs simple and uncluttered. Do not try to report too much on them. Use charts for illustration, and use words for explanation. Be concise. Most business people are busy. They want to get the information quickly and go on with their work. Do not bore them with your erudition. Get to the point, make it, and get out. Above all be accurate. Sloppy, careless, or just plain wrong data will destroy your credibility. If you are not good with numbers have someone who is check it before you publish. Those who disagree with you will be looking for a bad number. When they find one you can bet everyone will know about it. As my mother used to say to me when I was young, "if you cannot be smart in school, at least do neat work." If you cannot be smart with numbers, at least be accurate. Finally, be appropriate. Report what people want to know about, what you want them to know about, and what is important. Hopefully these will all be the same. It does more harm than good to report data that no one cares to know. All it does is clog your report, make it harder to follow, and add to the fatigue of the reader.

If your report is intended to do more than inform you still have to abide by the four characteristics just covered. But if you want to persuade, then you also must learn to lead the reader. Reports are commonly used to lead people in the organization to form a new opinion or to take some type of action. By leading I do not mean manipulate, misinform, or misrepresent. I am referring to the art of rhetoric, the business of persuasion. Rhetoric is the art of using language effectively. This means to create desired effects, which is just a roundabout way of saying persuade or sell. We tend to believe that most of our communication is informative in nature, when in fact more than 50 percent of it is aimed at persuasion. We are continually trying to convince people to believe in or do something. In order to survive and prosper it is often necessary to help people see things our way. There is nothing wrong with that in a large complex society, where there is such a wide range of attitudes, interests, values, and needs.

Persuasive efforts always proceed from a central idea which the audience can comprehend. Points are made in a logical, cause and effect sequence which leads the reader along in an orderly manner from the central idea toward the desired conclusion. To show cause and effect relationships it is usually necessary to have demonstrable, supporting evidence. This is where the power of numbers is so strong. The argument should proceed to the point at which the conclusion becomes self-evident. Two surrounding issues which help to shape your persuasive outline are the situation and the audience. Ancient rhetoricians studied only the discourse between the speaker and the audience. However, modern systems theories and holistic psychology have made us appreciate the impact of the environment on the persuasive event. You must consider how activities and events in the general area surrounding your point will influence it. If you are asking management to commit resources to a project, make sure that the financial condition of the organization will permit such an expenditure. If you want your boss to do something, make sure that it is something that top management does not oppose. The audience is, of course, the key issue and warrants its own special consideration.

Audiences are as diverse as the people who compose them. Organizations make the mistake of viewing their employees as a monolith. That is, they tend to communicate with their people as though there was only one personality for the whole group. Every individual has a different combination of interests, values, attitudes, and needs, and you can communicate effectively only if you take this into consideration. The questions are simple and straightforward. How interested are your readers in the subject? How much value do they place on it? Do they feel a need for it? What are their individual attitudes toward it?

Arising out of personality issues is the matter of preferred style. Assuming that your readers are interested enough to read the report, what format do they relate to best? Some people like a lot of detail. They want to see tables of numbers, sometimes out to two decimal places.

Other readers prefer the big picture. They will accept bar charts or trend lines which are not so specific but which give a quick impression of the situation. There is no way to persuade a big-picture person to plow through tables of numbers. Likewise, the accountant type feels insecure with only a slashing line across a graph. If you want people to read, comprehend, and react favorably to your reports you must do the courtesy of providing them with the data in the form they prefer.

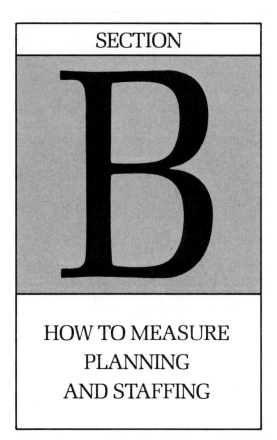

SECTION

B

HOW TO MEASURE PLANNING AND STAFFING

A Make or Buy Decision

THE FIRST INPUT

If the HR department is a system, then planning must be the first formal input. The planning section's job is to take data from the business plan, the strategic plan, and the marketplace and put it together in ways which meet certain needs of the organization. Like any other function, planning's role is somewhat predetermined by the style and values of the organization's management. I knew one corporation president in the electronics business who told me that there was no need to plan. He said, "we just stay very close to IBM, and whichever way they go we try to follow and leapfrog them occasionally." I suggested to him if such were the case he should create a spy unit instead of a planning function.

Planning has several purposes. The more central ones are to prepare data which assists management in making decisions about the future direction of the company, to help reduce uncertainty and risk by supplying pertinent information about the future, and to promote efficiency and effectiveness in the acquisition of human resources. While planners use numbers to communicate their story, there is more to the job than just statistics. A forward-looking group could involve themselves in auditing the job structure of the organization. You might believe that this is the compensation section's prerogative. However, what good does it do to project needs for jobs which are becoming obsolete, redundant, or inappropriate? Planning could try to come up with an algorithm to help it convert the business plan directly into a staffing plan. Planning could use its mathematical skills to work on other, nonplanning, assignments.

Planners have talents which are usually unique among human resources professionals. Most planners I know have a very restrictive view of their role in the organization. While they usually want to be closely involved with the decision makers, paradoxically they tend to be retiring types who do not thrust themselves into the action arenas. As a result, planning is most often a reactive operation which waits for someone to tell them what to work on. However, a planner can be a catalyst, and Grahn[1] describes how one planner did just that.

The planner in question converted the sales projection for the upcoming year into the number of invoices to be processed. Then, once she knew how many invoices could be processed per person per day, she showed the order-processing manager how many new people would be needed to handle the increased sales. Beyond the discovery of interesting information, she worked out a plan with the manager to increase the productivity of the order-processing function. The result was that the staffing growth curve leveled out somewhat in comparison to the sales growth curve.

Another approach to the planning function is to turn the planner into a coordinator. I once gave my planner the task of bringing together people from staffing, training, career development, and organizational development to create a model of effective management. The idea was that once we knew what kinds of skills, abilities, aptitudes, and interests were typical of an effective manager in our company, we would then be better able to recruit, counsel, and develop people according to their best fit in the organization and their maximum personal potential. The planner was excellent at this, for she had a better overview of the organization than did most and she was more experienced at handling the type of data which was collected.

PROFILING AND PROJECTING

One of the difficulties in trying to measure the work of planners is that their output is primarily a plan of the future. By definition, we will not know for 1, 3, or perhaps 5 years how accurate their predictions were. In addition no one is capable of predicting future events, and therefore it is not fair to blame the planner for unforeseeable events. It is impossible to measure the value of a long-term plan in the short term. Planners thus often feel frustrated because they cannot prove their worth with concrete evidence.

Basically, planning does two things. It profiles the current state of the employee population, and it projects future needs or conditions regarding that population. Since it is difficult to measure the effectiveness of projection, it might be better to look to profiling for evaluation purposes.

If the prime output of the planning group is a human resources plan, each year we will be able to measure whether or not the plan was published on time and whether it met any preset conditions and specifications. This is simple, obvious, and not very exciting. However, in order to produce the annual plan, certain data on the employee population must be developed. This data can be used for other projects which have some measurable short-term payoff.

The employees of an organization come in all sizes, ages, sexes, races, levels of education, experience, and performance. Planning can do distribution studies which correlate different variables. For instance, Fig. 5-1 shows a distribution of employees by age, performance (high ratings) level, and turnover. In this hypothetical example it is easy to see that there may be current and future problems. If you trace the profile of performance versus turnover you find that the high performers are between 25 and 40 years of age, and turnover is highest among that same age group. In fact, from 25 on, those two curves correlate almost perfectly. If you follow the age line you see that this organization has an aging population. The fact that age and high performance do not correlate at all is one more indicator of a problem. From this simple graph we can find enough work to keep the department and line management busy for some time.

There are many types of demographic studies which a planning section is well equipped to handle. It can study sourcing history for the staffing group. It usually has data which the EEO people could use. It can trace development patterns of identifiable employee groups such as MBAs. It can look at promotion patterns versus hiring patterns at middle management positions. There are few limitations put on planners by others. If planners will get involved in issues, such as those described above, it will be much easier to find ways to measure their productivity and effectiveness.

THE ACQUISITION PROCESS

The place where planning usually makes its mark is in its work with the staffing group. This is an extremely valuable function. The hiring decision is often taken too lightly; few organizations have stopped to figure out just how costly the decision to hire a new employee actually is.

The Upjohn Company has computed the career cost of an employee to be 160 times the first year's salary.[2] What is startling is that only 3 years ago Upjohn figured the career cost was 117 times the initial year's salary. This figure assumes a 30-year career. The fact that many employees do not stay with a company 30 years does not lessen the importance of the acquisition decision. Even if the average person spends less than 10 years with one organization, we cannot ignore the importance of the selection process.

Before buying equipment it is customary to detail the desired specifications and capabilities. Then a cost-benefit study is conducted to determine whether or not the equipment should be purchased. There are usually several choices to consider, since machines come with a range of speeds, weights, capacities, and options. The task is to select the one machine which is best suited to the operation.

It is the same with people. Each individual job applicant offers a unique combination of education, experience, aptitudes, skills, interests, needs, values, goals, and qualities. The selection process is not simple. Whether to fill a vacancy with an existing employee or to institute an outside search is the first and often one of the more critical decisions.

INTERNAL AND EXTERNAL SOURCES

The employment or staffing process has been thought of as the first step toward finding a replacement for an employee who has recently vacated a job. There are two potential sources of replacement: the outside labor pool and the existing internal work force. Often this second source is not fully utilized. As we saw in the previous chapter, the replacement process starts with a human resources planning system. When the skills inventory and succession planning subsystems are operating, by definition they are providing candidates for many openings. The need to look outside is diminished and the internal reservoir of applicants supplies qualified candidates.

In many organizations, the urge to seek candidates from outside the organization is more prevalent for higher-level openings than it is for lower-level ones. This is more often the case in young, fast-growing companies than in older, more stable organizations. Nevertheless, it occurs with enough frequency in both cases to support the generalization. Paradoxically, most organizational structures would suggest the opposite situation. Since they are pyramidal structures, the logic of mathematics tells us that there should be a larger number of employees below each level than there are above it. Hence, some, many, or in ideal cases all of those below a given opening might be qualified and interested in filling the spot. The planning system is responsible for sorting through the stockpile of available individuals and presenting those which most closely match the requirements of the position.

In the perfect situation, it might seem that we would want the planning system to be operating at a level of efficiency such that it could provide a fully qualified and intensely interested candidate from the internal work force for each position. As one job is vacated by an employee moving up to fill a higher-level job, the system provides a qualified candidate for that job. As the second and still lower-level job opened up, the system would provide yet another appropriate candidate. The process would cascade level by level until only entry-level jobs had to be filled from outside. The only exception would be unforeseeable or cataclysmic events. Examples could be an acquisition which would have to be staffed or a catastrophe such as a fire or a plane crash which would take several key people suddenly.

There is one problem with this idyllic process: filling all jobs from within leads to incestuous thinking. There has been a good bit of research into what is labeled "groupthink." Simply described, it is a situation where the individuals who make up a group achieve a state of shared experience and values to the point that they cease to function cognitively as individual minds and begin to accept, without challenging, virtually all ideas put forth by a member of the group. A high level of comfort, security, and certainty develops within the group. The "not-invented-here" syndrome ("If we didn't think of it, it must be worthless") takes over and blocks any novel ideas not presented by a group member. The amount of stimulus reception drops to a dangerously low level, and the group simply recycles the thoroughly processed ideas of the past. Such a case certainly speeds up decision making, but it completely shuts down the creative process. Recent American industrial history provides several textbook cases of this syndrome.

The railroad barons who fought each other for control of intercontinental traffic in the late 1800s concurrently developed a cadre of like-minded subordinates who carried on their myopic perception of the purpose of railroads. Within less than 100 years, while efficiency and innovation were the rule in Japanese and northern European rail systems, several major American railroads went bankrupt. A slightly newer, but nearly as ossified, industry was the automobile business between World War II and the late 1970s. Americans were selecting Volkswagens, and later Datsuns and Toyotas, by the hundreds of thousands while Detroit insisted it was only a passing fad. Despite over two decades of consistent buying patterns, the big three auto makers refused to accept the not-invented-here idea of small, economical, easy-handling cars. They very nearly choked themselves on the 2-ton sedan. It took 20 years of diminishing market share plus the action of a small group of sheikhs to finally convince the Detroit triumvirate that the V-8 was no longer the American dream.

A third example of incestuous thinking was the banking industry. As the post–World War II baby boom matured into the new home buyer boom in the early 1970s, the real estate market took off like a rocket. Banks began to lend for single- and multiple-family housing developments on a scale unprecedented in banking history. When a new financial animal called REIT (real estate investment trust) was born, banks leaped in to provide funds for developments which they would never have touched before. Their rationale was that they had been lending on real estate construction for over a century and that's what they were doing now. When the recession of 1974 hit, the facades of many an REIT collapsed, leaving banks with hundreds of millions of overleveraged projects suddenly in default. Subsequent losses contributed to the first bank failures since the Great Depression.

In each of the above cases, the problem developed not because of lack of capital, material, or equipment, but as a direct result of industrial hiring and promotion policies which said in effect, "give us more of the same." Incestuous value systems would not allow accurate perception of a changing world. The lesson for human resources planning systems is that they need to do more than provide bodies. The systems should be designed so they can differentiate between candidates in terms of their values, aptitudes, and creative abilities. The staffing problem of the 1980s is not only a matter of numbers, but more importantly, a matter of fit. Future shock has arrived: time frames have shrunk, the impact of decisions has increased, and risk has grown proportionately. Hence, selection must become a more scientific process.

Until we reach the point where the human planning system can provide for all needs, we will continue to depend on outside sources for applicants. Everyone knows that we can manage our internal resources to meet some of our replacement needs. However, many managers don't make any attempt to manage the outside resources. They simply accept what is apparent in their labor market and turn to it as needed. The problem is compounded when there is no central control over the use of outside media or sources. The message of the company goes out in a confusing and sometimes conflicting manner. Then problems over fees develop, public relations suffers, and budgets are overrun. In short, no one is in charge.

Sourcing is often spoken of as if it were solely an external event. Since applicants for jobs come from both internal and external pools, sourcing is obviously a two-sided job. Some companies have established a simple but effective means for bringing some order to the search function. They have set a quota, or a goal of filling a given percentage of jobs from internal sources. This goal may be a single, organizationwide number or it may be made up of subgoals by job group, level, or division. The goals take into consideration such factors as available internal and external pools, opportunity for training to help qualify people, organizational philosophy regarding commitment to employee security and growth, and availability of funds to pay outside fees. No matter how the program is set up, it accomplishes one very important objective. It prohibits line managers from launching their own quest and wreaking havoc with the organizational staffing program.

Another ally in the staffing business is Uncle Sam. While many decry the difficulty and sometimes the injustices which have come from EEO mandates, there are still positive aspects to be considered. Most organizations charge the human resources function with developing an affirmative action plan (AAP). Affirmative action plans are often little more than thick documents filed with an agency of the federal government in the hope that it will satisfy bureaucratic zeal for another year and allow the business to proceed unhindered. However, once the plan is created and ratified by management, it can be used as a control device. The first thing that should happen when an opening occurs is that the AAP is consulted. If it is a target job, that must be communicated. Obviously if that is the case sourcing is critical. The manager of staffing appoints a project leader who either monitors or takes charge of the search. A benevolent form of control is in effect and the job gets done.

One of the fundamental variables in the make or buy decision is cost. It takes money to run organizations, and it doesn't matter if it is a profit or a not-for-profit business. Money has to come from somewhere and it is usually in finite supply. The principle of most businesses has been: the less you spend on acquisition the more you can put into products or service. Yet ironically the acquisition process has a wider range of effects on the organization than is generally realized. The cost effectiveness of any given hire doesn't stop when the offer is accepted. That's actually when it starts, and it can be traced all the way through the new employee's career until the day that person becomes a turnover statistic. The issue of turnover cost really starts with selection. Turnover is as much a problem of the right hire as anything else. Some companies with historically high turnover rates have cut it 50 percent or more simply by working on improved selection programs. Granted, changes in the organization after the fact can hurt the best of selection efforts.

Nevertheless, a system which employs modern hiring tools and techniques can have a long-term positive impact.

In a study conducted in one company over a 3-year period, they found that in 8 out of 10 cases when they replaced a manager the new hire came in at a higher salary than the predecessor had earned. Along with that came all the acquisition costs, training costs, and learning curve losses—the loss in productivity which occurs while the new employee learns the job. Employees are investments. They should be treated as investments and not as expenses. They provide a return on the money spent to sustain them and thereby qualify as an investment. We spend a great deal of time in business studying potential returns on investments in capital equipment. However, we do not take that same care in scrutinizing a job candidate whose cost may be 10 to 50 times the cost of a new machine. A basic change of attitude toward the selection process is the first step in managing hiring costs.

THE FIRST MEASURE

In order to make an intelligent decision regarding the trade-offs between promoting from within or hiring from without we have to know the relative cost of each. In this chapter we will focus on what is often thought of as the first measure, cost per hire (C/H). Cost per hire applies whether we talk about internal or external sources. Internal placements do not require all the types of expenses that external sourcing does, but there are still costs and they need to be calculated.

At first blush we tend to think of C/H as the direct cost for advertising and agency fees. However, when you dig deeper you begin to realize the multitude of expenses generated by the replacement process. There are a half-dozen types of replacement expenses. They fall into the following categories:

Type	Expense
Source cost	Advertising and agency fees paid to generate applicants; hire and/or referral bonuses.
Staff time	Salary, benefit, and standard overhead cost of your staff to meet with the manager to discuss sourcing; work with the media and/or agency to commence the search; screen applications, call applicants in for interviews, interview and reference check; review candidates with the manager and schedule interviews; make or confirm the offer.
Management time	Salary, benefit, and standard overhead cost of the requesting department management to plan sourcing, discuss and interview candidates, and make a hiring decision and an offer.

Type	Expense
Processing cost	Manual or automatic data system cost of opening a new file; cost of medical exams; cost of employment and record verification (mail or telephone), security checks, etc.
Travel and relocation	Travel and lodging costs for staff and candidates; relocation costs.
Miscellaneous	Materials and other special or unplanned expenses. The cost of new employee orientation may be included or considered part of the training expenses.

In its simplest yet most complete form C/H could be expressed as shown in Formula S–1.

Cost per Hire

$$C/H = \frac{SC + ST + MT + PC + T\&R + Misc}{H} \qquad (S\text{–}1)$$

Obviously, many of the variables in the numerator are composed of more than one cost item. Many advertisements and agencies may have been used during a reporting period. They would have to be accumulated and summed to constitute SC. Staff and management times are labor costs multiplied by the number of applicants. System support, travel, relocation, and other costs all have to be added up to make a single large sum.

Since there is no generally accepted method of accounting for C/H you are free to choose from or add to the above list to create your own measure of it. While we do need a standardized method of calculating costs in all areas of human resources management so that we can compare data, there is also room for each of us to maintain a measurement system which serves the idiosyncratic needs of our organization.

Once you have decided which costs are going to be plugged into your C/H equation you then have a number of secondary decisions to make. Again, since there are no mandated accounting methods you are free to choose variables which meet your special requirements. Let us discuss each type of expense and the decisions that need to be made.

Source cost seems rather straightforward since the invoices from the advertisements and the fees from agencies are unequivocal. When you run one ad for one position it is easy to ascribe the cost of the ad to that hire. However, quite often combination ads are run which showcase two or more jobs. Sometimes a blanket ad calling for an unstated number of applicants is placed. An example of the first ad would be one which calls for supervisor of accounting, senior accountants, and bookkeepers. A sample of the second would be an ad stating simply "Assembler Wanted." In both cases, you are hoping for multiple hires from one ad.

In the assembler ad it is fairly simple to divide the ad cost by the number of assemblers hired to obtain an average ad cost. However, the accounting ad is a more complicated decision. Assuming you were to hire a supervisor, one senior accountant, and three bookkeepers from this ad, how would you apportion the cost among the five hires? Is it fair to divide the cost of the ad by five? That would make it look like it's as easy to hire supervisors as it is to hire bookkeepers. You could weight the charges by the salary level of each hire. In that case, should you use actual salary, entry-level salary, or the midpoint of the salary range?

Questions such as these become important if you are attempting a detailed analysis of your C/H. They are also issues if the cost of the ad must be charged back to user departments. There are occasions when two or more departments will agree to pool their resources to place a large ad for personnel who could be employed in several departments. A common example of this is the job of programmer. Today, many departments have programming staffs, and they are almost always in need of programmers. As an example, quite often a programmer may be able to function in both market research and corporate planning. If you are looking for junior and senior programmers for two different departments, the problem of cost allocation is compounded. It is important that you establish the ground rules ahead of time, because when there are dollars on the line manners seem to disappear. Also, you do not want one user to think that he was treated unfairly. If he does, he is not likely to be as cooperative the next time you want to optimize your return on the corporate advertising dollar. The issue in cases like these is not, "what is the right way?" There is no prescribed rule to follow. The question is, "what is the best way for all concerned at this time?" If you are going to calculate C/H over an extended period of time, which is the only worthwhile way, then you must have some consistency in your methodology. If you allocate costs one way this month and another way next month in an effort to keep everyone happy, your month-to-month results will not be comparable.

The calculation and allocation of staff time can also quickly become an indecipherable mess unless you establish an accounting method and stay with it. The simplest way to reduce this problem to a manageable and understandable variable is to introduce standard labor costing. By borrowing a leaf from manufacturing's book, you can determine the normal cost of an employee hour of work and set that as your standard rate. For example, an employment clerk's standard rate could be determined in the following manner:

Salary (converted to hourly rate)	$ 5.25
Benefits (30% of salary)	1.575
Overhead charge (space, equipment, etc.)	3.655
Total	$10.48

The standard rate you will apply to all staff time calculations where an employment clerk is involved is thus $10.48.

In time you will be able to develop an average number of hours that a clerk puts in on a given class of hires. Let us say, as an example, you find that the clerk spends 1½ hours on the average per direct labor hire. If you multiply $10.48 times 1½ the product is $15.72, which becomes the standard cost of an employment clerk's time for each direct laborer that the clerk assists in hiring. Multiply $15.72 times the number of hires that month and you have one component of the total month's cost of hiring. The same process is then applied to recruiters, receptionists, record clerks, and anyone else in your department who is involved in hiring. You may even choose to allocate a portion of the employment manager's time.

The process may need to be recomputed for different types or levels of jobs. It usually takes more time to hire managers than laborers. Hence, while your standard labor rates will not change, the amount of time each person devotes to the hire may change by job. Therefore, the multiplier changes. The most dramatic changes are usually with the recruiters. At the non-exempt level, recruiters may have to spend on average half an hour per applicant interviewing for each hire. At the exempt level, that could jump to 1½ or 2 hours per applicant. In addition, the number of applicants seen per hire may also vary significantly. This will strongly influence your C/H when calculated by job level. It takes time to set standard rates and to establish a realistic time multiplier. It is up to you to use what is the most appropriate to your situation. You are free to choose, so long as you are consistent.

The last thing to keep in mind when you employ standard labor rates is that rates change over time. The cost of a clerk or recruiter today is more than it was 5 years ago and surely less than it will be a year or two in the future. Periodically, you need to check your costs. It is usually sufficient to do this on an annual basis. To do it any more frequently would cause confusion in your monthly comparison of C/H statistics. If you kept loading in an amount for increases in salary or benefits on a quarterly basis, you would not be able to account for changes in C/H without laboriously modifying everything by introducing deflator factors. Remember, the real reason for measuring C/H and all the other dependent variables we will talk about is to find out if you are doing an effective job of managing the function. This is not an exercise in statistical precision, but a tool for managing.

The rules for computing staff time pretty much apply to figuring management time. It may be slightly more complex, depending on the level of detail you are after. There are many types and grades of managers in the departments you serve. From a practical standpoint it is probably not a good use of your time to calculate a standard rate for each of them. It might be sufficient to simply strike a rate for all middle-level managers and one for all upper-level managers. If even that is too unwieldy to manage, do whatever will work and still be representative of the time and effort involved.

Processing costs are the most frequently overlooked expense in the equation. I use the term here to cover all the manual and automated record keeping and computing support used during the hiring process. I also include the costs of testing and medical work of any kind plus the material and transmittal costs of reference checks and employment verifications.

Applicant tracking systems are becoming commonplace in large employment departments. The impracticality of manually maintaining control of hundreds of applications which are constantly moving in, out, and around the department has caused the development of automated systems. Some systems are little more than record keepers which allow for a quick lookup. Others are quite sophisticated packages which track the whereabouts and history of each application. They may include a requisition tracking system and be tied into the job-posting system. These marvels of modern electronics can cost $100,000 to purchase or several thousand dollars per month to rent. As such, they need to be entered into the equation.

Other support expenses are selection testing, whether it be a simple typing test or a complex battery of psychological tests. Many companies are involved in medical screening and examinations, and so those costs must be included. Finally, either before or shortly after a hire is made there are verification processes that must take place. Past employment is usually checked, claims of college degrees are authenticated, and background investigations for bonding or security clearance are often necessary. These activities have costs associated with them and should not be ignored. When you add up the costs of support activities for the first time, you will probably be amazed at the amount of money that is spent.

Expenses associated with travel and relocation are significant. For example, a managerial candidate flown from the midwest to either coast, fed and lodged for a day or two, and flown home can easily cost the company several hundred dollars. And that's only for the first trip of one candidate. By the time you do that for two or three, bring the finalist's spouse out to look over the territory, and top it off with a house-hunting trip, you have watched a couple of thousand dollars disappear. And you haven't even begun relocation yet. There are many relocation firms which have published studies showing the cost of moving a family can easily run over $10,000, not counting third-party house purchase expenses.

Although we can't ignore travel and relocation costs, their treatment deserves special attention. Quite often management positions are filled without incurring any significant travel or relocation expenses. Then all of a sudden you may spend $15,000 or more on one hire. If you simply throw that one in with the ten preceding it where you may have spent less than $1000 total, the ensuing average C/H will be skewed. The number will be misleading and totally nonindicative of what has happened over the last eleven hires.

The $15,000 must be added to the total cost of hiring for the month. However, it will probably be appropriate to report two sets of figures. One would be those hires which did not require relocation. The other would be those in which there were relocations. Not only is this more truthful, it provides management with an appreciation for the impact of relocation expenses on the bottom line. Your job is not only to show management how effectively you are managing your department, it is also imperative to show them how the job could be be done better. If you can come up with a plan to avoid having to hire people who require relocation, you can probably get support for it.

Beyond the five categories of expenses we have just covered there is a sixth catchall category. Some companies have employee referral bonus programs wherein they pay current employees a bounty if they bring in qualified applicants who are subsequently hired. Some desperate organizations have gone so far as to offer hiring bonuses to people who come in directly without going through an agency. Whether this is a short-term or long-term phenomenon is irrelevant. There will always be some kind of special expense which eludes the best plan. The point is simply to keep your eyes open and be sure that it is included.

The allocation of employee orientation costs is a question which currently does not have a definitive answer. Some HR managers think it is a cost of hire since it usually occurs before the person actually assumes the job. Even if it comes a week or a month later, they believe it should be charged to hiring because the information presented is aimed strictly at easing the induction of the new person into the organization. Another opinion is that orientation takes place after the hire and therefore is part of an individual's training. To date, this argument has not been resolved. In my opinion, until we adopt a generally accepted set of accounting principles for our field, it is a moot point. Account for it on either side and let it stand by itself. The only rule that always applies is: be consistent.

BREAKING IT DOWN

The true value of the measurement system becomes apparent only when you dig into a dependent variable such as cost per hire. The bottom line number: $C/H = \$X$ for a given month, is the starting point for what can be a very enlightening tour of the employment function. Whether you have an automated or a manual system you can set it up to extract a wide variety of C/H subsets. You can divide C/H by any of the types of expenses we discussed above. Furthermore, you can mix and match those independent variables in just about any combination. The net effect is a chance to discover in great detail just where you are being extraordinarily effective and where you can improve.

It is very easy to cut your C/H by source. You can compare the average C/H using the cost of advertising versus the cost of agencies. You can throw in other sources, such as employee referrals, and make multiple comparisons. Another fundamental cut is level. You can look at C/H by exempt, non-exempt, and hourly wages. You can cut it finer by laying it out according to salary grade. If you combine level with job groups you can look at the difference between the C/H of entry-level, junior, and senior programmers, for instance. Of course, in order to be able to make those cuts you have to remember to collect that data at the time of hire. The more you want to manipulate the data, the more it helps to have a computer. Nevertheless, if care is taken in designing a manual logging system, a great deal of valuable information can be generated with any measurement system.

Figure 5.1 shows a three-dimensional analysis matrix. It is a graphic way of considering the many subsets of cost per hire that are obtainable.

Each block within the matrix contains the cost per hire of a given type of employee in a given department using a given source. For example, block 1 would display the cost of hiring an exempt employee for department A using advertising. Block 7 would show non-exempt employee costs for department A using agencies. Moving back into the third dimension, block 50 would show costs for hourly workers in department B using nonprofit agencies.

Obviously, all costs cannot be illustrated this way. Each department's data would have to be pulled out of the matrix and put on a separate report sheet. The point is simply to show how the addition of

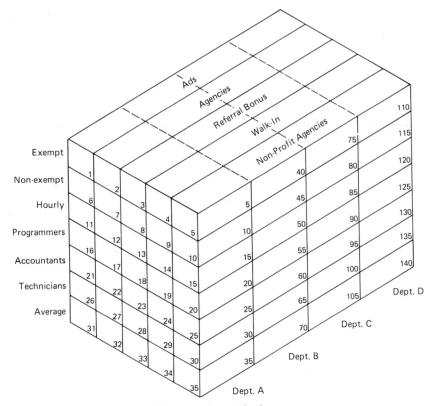

Figure 5.1   Three-Dimensional Analysis Block

each variable—i.e., a department—geometrically generates several other measures. Once again we are reminded that it is not a question of whether we can measure our work or not. It is only a matter of choosing which outcome, from a field of nearly infinite size, we want to measure.

1. Source Analysis.   In the analysis block, standard costs for staff and management time, travel, relocation, and other costs were taken as givens. The outcomes, the costs in each cell, were only the sourcing costs. The process of holding certain costs constant and calculating certain others is a good way to isolate and emphasize trends. The basic equation is seen in Formula S–2.

Source Cost per Hire

$$SC/H = \frac{AC + AF + RB + NC}{H} \qquad (S\text{–}2)$$

where   AC = advertising costs, total monthly expenditure [e.g., $28,000]

AF = agency fees, total month (e.g., $19,000)

RB = referral bonuses, total paid (e.g., $2300)

NC = no-cost hires, walk-in, nonprofit agencies, etc. (i.e., $0)

H = Total hires (e.g., 119)

EXAMPLE

$$SC/H = \frac{\$28,000 + \$19,000 + \$2300 + \$0}{119}$$

$$= \frac{\$49,300}{119}$$

$$= \$415$$

The basic formula can be varied by changing total hires (H) to include only exempt hires (EH), or non-exempt hires (NEH):

$$SC/H = \frac{AC + AF + RB + NC}{EH} \quad \text{or} \quad SC/H = \frac{AC + AF + RB + NC}{NEH}$$

Once you have the basic formula you can change the denominator to any group of hires and recompute cost per source just for that group.

For reporting purposes it is enlightening to show the comparative costs of each source of hire. To do that, simply separate the variables in the numerator and do separate computations:

$$SC/H = \frac{AC}{H} \quad \frac{AF}{H} \quad \frac{RB}{H} \quad \frac{NC}{H}$$

A sample report based on this type of cost analysis is shown in Fig. 5.2.

2. Special Recruiting Programs.   It is useful to evaluate the costs and outcomes of ongoing programs on a periodic basis. For college recruitment programs or national recruiting campaigns the costs can be identified and separate calculations performed. Staff and management time may be included or not, depending on your objective:

$$SC/H = \frac{AC + AF + T \& R (+ ST + MT)}{H}$$

The result can be compared to other methods of recruitment as one input to a cost-benefit analysis.

(a) April: Cost of hires by source, in dollars

	Agency			Ads			Employee referrals			Nonprofit other	
	Number	Total cost	Cost per hire	Number	Total cost	Cost per hire	Number	Total cost	Cost per hire	Number	Cost
Exempt	6	47,500	7,916	8	24,375	3,047	5	1,500	300	1	00
Non-exempt	1	624	624	24	10,078	420	24	2,400	100	9	00
Total	7	48,124	6,875	32	34,453	1,077	29	3,900	134	10	00

Total number hired	Total cost	Cost per hire
20	73,375	3,669
58	13,102	226
78	86,477	1,109

(b) Year to date: Cost of hire by source, in dollars

	Agency			Ads			Employee referrals			Nonprofit other	
	Number	Total cost	Cost per hire	Number	Total cost	Cost per hire	Number	Total cost	Cost per hire	Number	Cost
Exempt	21	83,512	3,977	28	43,282	1,546	16	4,800	300	3	00
Non-exempt	8	2,843	355	91	26,270	289	69	6,900	100	17	00
Total	29	86,355	2,978	119	69,552	584	85	11,700	138	20	00

Total number hired	Total cost	Cost per hire
68	131,594	1,935
185	36,013	195
253	167,607	662

Year to year	
1978	712
1979	662

Figure 5.2 Source Cost per Hire Report (a) April (b) Year to Date

3. Interviewing Costs. You already know how to calculate standard labor costs for your staff and for outside management. Observations will disclose how long, on the average, each interview takes. The cost of interviewing (C/I) as a component of the total cost is a simple, two-step process:

Step 1: Interviewing Cost

$$C/I = \frac{ST + MT}{I} \qquad (S-3)$$

where   ST = staff time, total staff time spent interviewing [e.g., $10.60 per hour standard cost times a half-hour per interview times number interviewed]

   MT = management time, total management time spent interviewing (e.g., management time is based on a $24.60 hour standard labor cost times 1 hour per interview times number interviewed)

   I = number interviewed, total number of applicants interviewed (e.g., 295)

EXAMPLE

$$C/I = \frac{\$1563 + \$7257}{295}$$
$$= \frac{\$8820}{295}$$
$$= \$29.90$$

Step 2: Source Cost per Hire (per Interview)

$$SC/H = \frac{IC + AC + AF + RB + NC}{H} \qquad (S-4)$$

where   IC = total monthly interviewing costs, by using the formula of cost per interview to calculate total interviewing costs [e.g., $8820]

   AC = advertising costs, total monthly advertising expenditures (e.g., $28,000)

   AF = agency fees, total monthly agency fees paid [e.g., $19,000]

   RB = referral bonuses, total monthly referral bonuses paid (e.g., $2300)

   NC = no-cost hires, nonprofit agencies, etc. (e.g., $0)

EXAMPLE

$$SC/H\ (P/I) = \frac{\$8820 + \$28,000 + \$19,000 + \$2300 + 0}{119}$$

$$= \frac{\$58,120}{119}$$

$$= \$488$$

This example reflects the cost of the fact that, while there were only 119 hires, it was necessary to interview 295 applicants.

SPECIAL EVENT ANALYSIS

At some point in their career most staffing managers find themselves in a position of having to perform some special recruitment magic. It may be there is an immediate need for a large number of a certain type of employee, such as assembly workers. Or perhaps a given job group —programmers, for example—is in extremely short supply. Whatever the particular need, the manager may decide to conduct some type of special event designed to recruit a relatively large number of people in a very short time. This may take the form of an open house. Open houses are often day-long or evening events where both recruiters and line managers are on hand to expedite interviews and offers. A media blitz takes place for a week or so in advance of the event. Refreshments are often served, and door prizes or favors may even be given away. Essentially, the manager marshals all the company's resources and concentrates them on this one important day, with the hope that it will attract a large number of qualified candidates and fill most of the open requisitions.

When the event is over, the staffing manager will want to evaluate its effectiveness, based on the ROI. There is a simple method for calculating that which consists of four steps.

1. Make a list of all expenses on the left side of a sheet of paper. These include ad costs, management time costs for both the personnel staff and the involved line department, refreshments, door prizes (if used), and all other types of costs shown on Formula S–1. Total these at the bottom of the column.

2. Write the number of people hired (assuming in this case they are all of one type—for example, programmers) on the right side of the page. If you were looking for several unrelated job groups, such as accountants, technicians, and secretaries, it will be difficult to precisely divide the costs among the different types. If

separate ads for each type were run those could be assigned to each group. General expenses, such as refreshments, could be prorated according to the number of applicants for each job group. Therefore, you may have to prepare more than one analysis sheet.

3. Divide the total expenses by the total number of hires to obtain C/H for this event. This tells the manager what the absolute ROI was, but it does not tell if it is better or worse than the cost would have been using conventional means. In order to answer that question one more step is required.

4. Referring to the most current data on cost per hire for similar jobs, compare the open house C/H to the staffing department's monthly report on cost per hire. This final step tells the manager if the open house hires were less expensive or more expensive hires than those obtained by the other method. Normally, well-planned and executed special events yield a better C/H than standard methods. Focused attention and high levels of cooperation usually yield high ROIs. Even if the event's C/H is higher there is a trade-off in time spent. In a few days of preparation and action such an event usually fills more open positions than weeks of standard recruiting. If there is a premium for quick results, the special event almost always delivers.

On the question of hire quality, we have found that special events produce applicants of about equal caliber to those obtained through conventional methods. Ways of assessing the quality of hires will be discussed in the next chapter.

SUMMARY

Evaluating the cost effectiveness of the employment process is one of the easier judgments to make. Costs are mostly visible in the form of invoices for advertisements, fees, and travel. The less apparent expenses, such as the cost of someone's time, can be found quickly. The only difficulties human resources staffs consistently complain of is their inability to get their hands on the cost data. In some companies the bills are sent directly to the hiring manager for approval and then to accounts payable for payment, bypassing the personnel office completely. When that is the habitual pattern, a deal can be made with the accounting department.

Sometimes the accountants receive bills on which they have little or no information. They spend a good deal of their time tracking down the source of the bill or the person who submitted it in order to get an explanation or an approval signature. If you are being bypassed, tell the accountants that if they will pass all employment-related bills to you, you will verify the amounts, relate them to a given event, and obtain the necessary approvals. The controller will thank you for taking an onerous, time-consuming task off the accounting staff's backs. And you will then be in control of the process, rather than a passive spectator.

No human resources department can claim to operate efficiently if it does not know how much it is spending to hire people. Acquisition costs are important no matter whether you are talking about machines or employees. Fortunately, these costs are easily obtainable, powerful tools for proving that you are maximizing the organization's recruiting ROI.

Do You Want
Speed or Quality?

TIME TRAP

There are a number of factors in the employment process which are not direct cost measures. This does not mean that they are worthless as indicators of the performance level of the staffing department. Indirect measures can be important if they are used appropriately. Some issues in human resources work do not readily lend themselves to cost analysis. Effectiveness is a term which goes beyond issues of productivity or efficiency. To assess the effectiveness of any function, we need measures which deal with time, quality, and quantity. In Chapter 2 we pointed out that indirect measures can be converted to direct measures through various simple processes, yet indirect measures have a value all their own.

All measures, whether direct or indirect, can be used for at least two broad purposes. One is to help you manage and control your organization, and the other is to deal with people outside of your group. You may be called on to report your activities and results, or you may be required to defend yourself against criticism of your work. The staffing department is often accused of taking too long to develop job candidates. By computing how long it has taken to find and refer qualified candidates and how long it normally takes to fill open requisitions, you will be able to demonstrate that the claims are unfounded. Some managers like to have an unreasonably large number of candidates from which to choose. In their zeal to defend their lack of decisiveness, they may claim that they never see more than one or two qualified people. By referring to your applicant tracking system you can prove that, on the average, they had perhaps 6 to 10 decent candidates from which to select.

Let us pause at this point to establish once and for all a fundamental issue regarding the qualifications of the job applicants you refer to management for interviewing. If you have dealt with the types of criticisms of timeliness and quantity we have just discussed, you may then have to answer for the quality of your referrals. Indecisive, overworked, or mediocre managers may concede upon proof that you have met the tests of time and volume. Then, in a face-saving attempt, they may accuse you of referring inferior or unacceptable individuals. There is only one way to effectively deal with this, and your position must be absolutely inflexible. You only refer one type of applicant: a qualified applicant. You do not send out teasers, loss leaders, straw men, shock troops, or any other type of quasi-qualified or unqualified individuals. If you ever admit to offering management anything but a suitable candidate you will destroy your credibility and undermine your position forever. There is absolutely no other stance to take. Period; end of discussion.

In addition to evaluating the effectiveness of recruiters, you will need to evaluate your staffing systems and procedures. For example, just about every employment function has a job-posting system, which can be reviewed both in terms of usage and results. Processing times for applications and records can be checked periodically. All the various routines, methods, programs, and procedures which support staffing can be tracked and checked. It is, as always, only a matter of choosing which processes are worth your time to measure.

Basically, there are two time issues in the recruitment process. One has to do with how long it takes to develop qualified candidates and refer them to management for interview. We call this *response time.* This is the period over which you have the most control. The other is how long it takes to fill a job requisition. We call this *time to fill.* Once you refer an applicant, your degree of control begins to lessen. We will discuss the recruiter's responsibility after referral when we come back to this second issue.

Response time is defined as the time from the day you have in hand a signed, approved job requisition, to the day on which you call or visit the requesting manager and announce that you have at least one qualified candidate ready to be interviewed. This is an important issue. Although it does not mean that you have completed your assignment, it does show how quickly your procurement system works. Formula S–5 shows the response time calculation. In this case it is not a ratio, as we are accustomed to working with in cost measures, but a subtraction problem.

Response Time

$$RT = RD - RR \qquad \text{(S–5)}$$

where RT = response time
RD = date of first qualified candidate referred for interview
(e.g., January 22)*
RR = date of receipt of job requisition (e.g., January 4)

EXAMPLE

$$RT = 22 - 4$$

$$= 18 \text{ days}$$

By adding total days to respond and dividing by total hires, an average response time results.

This formula came in very handy for me one day. I received a call from high-ranking person in our company who proceeded to chew me out for the alleged slow response time of my recruiters. Since I did not know offhand what our current rate was for the job classification he was angry about, I told him I would look into it and get back to him. After he hung up I went to the lady who kept our applicant tracking system and asked her for the log she used. I was frankly concerned that there might be some justification for the complaint because the jobs he pointed out were computer programmers. At the time programmers were a very scarce commodity in our marketplace. I was hoping that we had at least maintained a reasonable response rate over the year. The worst situation would be if each month our time to respond had increased. Within a few minutes I was able to draw out of the log the average reponse time for programmers over the past 10 months. I constructed a simple chart and plotted the results on it. An example of what it looked like is shown in Fig. 6.1.

As you can see, it showed unequivocally that the recruiters were doing a superb job. In a bad market they were managing to respond more quickly each month throughout the year. You can imagine my pleasure when I called the gentleman back and said, "John, I don't know

---

*If the referral date is in a different month than the requisition date simply count the intervening dates. For example,

$$RT = \text{February 20} - \text{January 4}$$
$$= 27 \text{ days in January} + 20 \text{ days in February}$$
$$= 47 \text{ days}$$

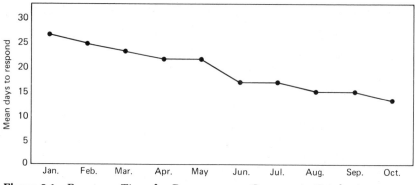

Figure 6.1 Response Time for Programmers (January to October)

where you are getting your data, but my records show that our current response time is only about 14 days. Over the year it has gotten better, not worse." He replied that he found my numbers rather hard to believe. So I suggested he come over to my office and take a look at the books for himself. To make a long story short he came over, and when he saw the evidence, he stormed out of my office vowing vengeance on his managers. I learned later that he went back to his department and verbally assaulted his staff for lying to him. The problem had been that they were not making their schedules and were blaming it on staffing for not filling the numerous open requisitions.

You probably know what was happening. The managers were claiming that, for a wide variety of highly imaginative reasons, they did not have time to see the candidates we were referring. By the time they came back to us and said they were ready, the candidates had found jobs in other departments in our company or in other companies. The recruitment process had to start all over again. This resulted in jobs being open for many weeks and work not getting done. When put under the gun by John, they sought a scapegoat in the staffing department.

This is a fairly typical example of how the human resources department can be given the blame for a line department's problems. The lesson is clear. If I had not had the data to set the record straight, I probably would have had to take the blame for the problem. I call that bag holding—one manager will walk into another manager's office and make an accusation. In effect, the accused is handed a bag of garbage. Unless the accused can muster a defense based on facts, that person will usually have to take the bag. Personnel staff members have more than their share of garbage bags tossed through their doors. If they have a measurement system which demonstrates their performance, they can tell the bearer to take the garbage and put it where it belongs.

The second time issue which was mentioned earlier in the chapter was time to fill. The layperson has the notion that the recruiting process is a relatively simple matter. The perception is that a requisition is delivered to staffing, an ad is run, applicants are screened, and a few are selected for interviews by management. In fact, the process has about 30 separate steps to it. Time to fill measures the total number of days between the delivery of an approved requisition to staffing and the arrival of the newly hired employee ready to go to work. The calculation is exactly the same as it was for response time. The only difference is that the referral date (RD) is replaced by the start date (SD). Start date refers to the day the new hire reports for work. Thus, Formula S–6 for time to fill is start date minus receipt date.

Time to Fill

$$TF = RR - SD \qquad (S–6)$$

where   TF = time to fill the job
RR = date the requisition is received (e.g., January 4)
SD = date the new hire starts work (e.g., March 10)

EXAMPLE

$$TF = January\ 4 - March\ 10$$
$$= 65$$

A staffing manager who is looking for opportunities to improve the time to fill record of recruiters does not have to look hard. I said above that there are about 30 steps to the recruitment and selection process. A system can be set up to track the more significant points in that 30-step process. Any large-volume recruitment function should have an applicant and requisition tracking system. Computerized systems are available at relatively low costs. With such a process in place, an ongoing audit of efficiency is easy. Figure 6.2 is an example of how one might look.

Select the key checkpoints that you want the system to record. In this example, which is a manual logging system, I have chosen 10 checkpoints. This system can be programmed to run as part of the core function of an applicant tracking system.

There is another way to record these events. In the event date cell put the number of days or elapsed time since the last event. For example, on the first requisition from manager J. Jones the line would read:

Event	1	2	3	4	5	6	7	8	9	10
Date	9/1	1	7	5	6	9	6	1	7	33

Requesting manager	Event* and date									
	1	2	3	4	5	6	7	8	9	10
J. Jones	9/1	9/2	9/9	9/14	9/20	9/29	10/5	10/6	10/13	11/15
F. Koontz	9/2	9/4	9/11	9/17	9/22	9/30	10/7	10/9	10/10	11/1
L. Smith	9/7	9/8	9/16	9/22	9/30	10/9	10/20	10/21	10/30	11/15
G. Mack	9/7	9/9	9/19	9/30	10/15	10/25	11/10	11/12	11/18	12/7
E. Kieffer	9/8	9/9	9/15	9/30	10/9	10/16	11/5	11/7	11/14	1/2

*Event numbers:
1—Requisition received; 2—Sourcing started; 3—First applicant responds; 4—First screening;
6—First management interview; 7—Hiring decision made; 8—Offer made; 9—Offer accepted/
rejected; 10—New employee starts work.

Figure 6.2   Hiring Track

Event 1 is the receipt of the requisition; the starting date for the
process. You could put 0 for elapsed time. However, the starting date
is more worthwhile. Since event 2 took place on 9/2, there is 1 day of
elapsed time and the number 1 is entered. Event 3 was on 9/9 which
is 7 days later, and so on across the line. This approach has the advantage of showing immediately how much time has been lost between
steps. For the manager who is looking for places to cut response time
and time to fill the delays are very apparent. The largest opportunities
are at events 3, 6, 9, and 10.

In place of requesting manager, the job title can be entered. In a
computerized system you would have both because you do not have the
space limitations of a manual log. When you have too little space, the
best solution is to show job title and department number.

Time is the enemy of the ambitious recruiter. By keeping track of
response time and time to fill the recruiter and the manager will know
for themselves how they are doing. They will also be able to defend
themselves if necessary. Finally, they will be able to go to line management with the facts to obtain cooperation in speeding up the process.

REFERRAL RATE

One large company in the northwest for many years was the major
employer in its region. The staff members had become accustomed to
taking their time in recruiting, and enjoyed the luxury of having many

applicants for each vacancy. As a result, managers developed the habit of looking at as many as 10 candidates before they made a hiring decision. Late in the 1970s other organizations around the country began to see the advantages of locating plants in the northwest. Within a year or two, several large- and medium-sized plants had been built within 15 miles of the *grande dame.* Suddenly there was competition for qualified personnel. However, the managers of the first company continued their habit of waiting for staffing to produce 7 to 10 candidates. When they began to go for weeks without filling jobs they complained loudly to staffing. At last they heard what they had been told before: the old game had changed. They could no longer expect more than two or three candidates for most positions. For certain jobs, they would be lucky to have one.

As market conditions change, referral rates generally change accordingly. In the case just described, management's expectations and practices had to change if they wanted to fill their jobs. One of the ways that the staffing manager can keep on top of the change is to compute a referral ratio. In order to avoid confusion with the RR symbol from the response time formula, we use RF to stand for the referral ratio and we call it the referral factor. The ratio is shown in Formula S–7.

Referral Factor

$$RF = \frac{R}{O} \qquad (S\text{--}7)$$

where   RF = referral factor, relationship of candidates to openings
        R = number of candidates referred for interview (e.g., 76)
        O = number of openings (e.g., 22)

EXAMPLE

$$RF = \frac{76}{22}$$
$$= 3.5$$

This data can be collected by job group or work unit to show how many qualified candidates, on the average, are being developed. A variation on this formula is to substitute hires for openings. All openings do not result in hires. Sometimes conditions change between the time that an approved job requisition arrives and a hire can take place. The difference is subtle, but perhaps meaningful in some situations. A realistic referral factor will always be a combination of management demand and market conditions. No matter which one predominates, the staffing manager should know what the ratio is in case a good defensive strategy is needed.

JOB-POSTING SYSTEM

In the career development chapter of Section E we will deal with the job-posting system as part of the career development effort. At this point we will look at it solely from an administrative standpoint.

Three views of job posting are the employees' use of the system, the rate of hire generated by the system, and the role of the system in the total hiring scheme. Each perspective provides opportunities for measurement.

Periodically jobs are posted for employees to see and apply for. In terms of this discussion, it does not matter which job levels are posted or how long jobs are left on the list. Posting systems vary widely among industries and in different parts of the country. Management philosophy, union status, and other issues dictate how a system will be run. So long as the system rules do not change, valid measurements can be conducted over time. No matter what the style of the system is, the first question to ask is, "how are people responding to it?" When you post a job, what happens? Are you flooded with employees anxious to transfer? Does anyone at all show up? The basic measurement is the job-posting response rate (JPR), which indicates how many responses are received per job posting. Formula S–8 shows the measures used to calculate JPR.

Job-Posting Response Rate

$$JPR = \frac{A}{PJ} \qquad (S–8)$$

where   JPR = job-posting response rate
   A = number of applications received at the job-posting desk (e.g., 348)
   PJ = number of posted jobs (e.g., 65)

EXAMPLE

$$JPR = \frac{348}{65}$$

$$= 5.4 \text{ applications per posting}$$

People may apply for several jobs simultaneously, realizing that they can only be successful in obtaining one of them. Nevertheless, count applications rather than applicants, because this tells what the system is generating. The fact that some people are chronic applicants or have other idiosyncratic reasons for applying is an issue outside the system itself. Sorting through hundreds of applications in search of multiples from one person is just not worth the effort and pulling those few out of the pile will not make a significant difference in the numbers.

Job posting, if monitored, can yield much more than a list of applicants for open positions. Assume that there is a flood of applicants for a particular job or for all jobs. What could that mean? The answer can be found somewhere among the reasons people apply for transfer. A few are

- Desire for advancement
- Escape from a bad supervisor
- Disinterest in current job (boredom)
- Escape from a bad interpersonal situation (coworkers)
- Better pay
- Move to a new location (geographic)
- Change of shift
- Family or health problems

An analysis of the source of applications and the reasons given by applicants often help pinpoint an organizational problem. If the people who run the posting system develop credibility with the employees, they will tell your job counselors the real reasons for their application. Poor supervision, boring jobs, unsafe or unhealthy environments, inequitable pay, or other sources of employee unrest will surface. Then you will have a chance to investigate and decide whether or not the complaints are reasonable.

Assume that very few employees respond to postings. What could that mean? It may mean

- There is a consistent history of rejection in favor of outside applicants
- There is no visible support from management
- There are threats from supervisors about applying for other positions in the company
- Your department has done a substandard job of dealing with applicants
- Only low-level jobs are posted

In my experience, all of the above occur. But unless you are monitoring your responses, you will never become aware of potentially serious organizational problems. Consider as just one example the consequences of supervisors threatening people who apply for posted jobs. Immediately you recognize the possibility of unfair labor practice charges or discrimination suits. Besides playing the traditional role of a transfer mechanism, the job-posting system can also be an early warning device. If you have your antenna up and scanning, you just might see something coming over the horizon in time to intercept it.

There are variations on the basic JPR formula, one of which is how to calculate how many posted jobs were responded to, as in Formula S–9.

Job-Posting Response Factor

$$JPRF = \frac{PJR}{PJ} \qquad (S-9)$$

where   JPRF = Ratio of jobs posted to jobs responded to
         PJR = number of posted jobs responded to (e.g., 58)
          PJ = number of posted jobs (e.g., 65)

EXAMPLE

$$JPR = \frac{58}{65}$$
$$= 89.2\%^*$$

This gives you a picture of the spread of responses. In the first formula, you may have a large number of applications per posting. But, they might be for only certain jobs. Averages can be deceiving, so there is a measure in statistics called *standard deviation.* It tells you how broadly the numbers are spread from the mean. In a sense, that is the type of function which this measure performs. It tells you whether or not all of your jobs are being applied for. If the number is less than 100% you can make a note of which jobs are not drawing applicants. If those jobs continually fail to turn up any interest, you can look into the reasons and do whatever is appropriate.

Another way to track responses is by job. It may be worthwhile to know which jobs are drawing the largest number of applicants. This is not discovered by use of a formula; it is a logging task. You can set up a log, either manually or automatically, that looks like Fig. 6.3. Applica-

---

*The maximum percentage can never exceed 100%.

Job name or number	Number of applicants
Accounting clerk	11111 11111 1
Assembler II	11111 11111 11111 11
Senior buyer	11111 111
Personnel representative	11

Figure 6.3 Applicant Log

tions are tallied by job and the story tells itself. Again, followup will uncover the reasons for abnormally high or low responses.

The second test of the job-posting system takes the process of application one step further. It deals with the number of hires or placements which result from the system. The formula used here is called the job-posting hire rate (JPH). It is seen in Formula S–10.

Job-Posting Hire Rate

$$JPH = \frac{H}{JP} \tag{S–10}$$

where   JPH = percentage of jobs filled through job posting
H = Number of hires made from internal applicants (e.g., 54)
JP = Number of jobs posted (e.g., 65)

EXAMPLE

$$JPH = \frac{54}{65}$$
$$= 83.1\%$$

This measure follows the same logic as the job-posting response ratio and carries the process to its conclusion. If a high rate of response is coupled with an equally high rate of hire the system would appear to be fulfilling its mission. If both factors are not in an acceptable range it is a sign that the system should be reviewed for defects. This is what people in business like to call the bottom line. After all is said and done, what was the result? Obviously the objective is to fill a large percentage of the posted jobs. You may not want to fill every position from internal sources, for this could lead eventually to the types of organizational incest described earlier. Fortunately, most industries have learned their lesson and they no longer expect or want all promotions to come up through the system.

Some companies set targets or goals for internal replacement rates. This is probably a healthy thing to do. It lets everyone know what the expectation is. If it is well communicated, employees will understand and support it. A formula for measuring that is called the internal hire rate, shown in Formula S–11.

Internal Hire Rate

$$IH = \frac{IA}{H}$$

(S–11)

where   IH = percent of jobs filled internally
IA = jobs filled by internal applicants (e.g., 49)
H = total hires (e.g., 76)

EXAMPLE

$$IH = \frac{49}{76}$$
$$= 64.5\%$$

I know of one company which encourages supervisors and managers to support the job-posting program by a cost transference mechanism. It works like this. Department A decides to accept the transfer request of an employee from department B. A then must pay B, through a cross charge, $X to cover the cost incurred by B to recruit a replacement. The amount is predetermined at the beginning of the year based on the average cost of hiring either an exempt or non-exempt employee. If B replaces their lost employee from another internal source then the charge passes to that department. Eventually, whoever has to go outside for a replacement is compensated for that expense. If the last department in line does not choose to replace, it still gets the money as a reward for having developed a good employee and for having found a way to operate more efficiently.

Job-posting measures are a good example of the inherent value in measurement. These seemingly secondary issues yield information well beyond what appears on the surface. In the process of obtaining data on one subject, the procedure and the results cause another set of questions to be asked. Gradually the holistic, interrelated, systems nature of the human resources function reveals itself. Time and again we will see how one process connects with another. In this one small series of job-posting measures we have discovered how job counselors are connected to affirmative action, employee relations, compensation, and labor relations. As we work through each of the main functions of human resources, the real reward for measurement will become overwhelmingly clear.

RECRUITING EFFICIENCY

In order to describe the performance of a recruiter we have to look at more than just how many applicants the recruiter helped to turn into hires. Some recruiters believe that hires are the sole criteria of their efficiency. However, like everyone else, recruiters work in a group as part of a team. How they handle their total job responsibilities is as important as the number of hires they effect.

I believe that it is better to measure recruiters as a group rather than as individuals. This principle holds true wherever possible for other functions as well. If people feel that they are constantly under the gun to come up with good numbers, they are liable to succumb to the temptation and give you what you seem to want: numbers rather than results. When employees start to manufacture numbers the system is worse than useless, it is fraudulent. Treat your recruiters as a team. Pool their data and report their results as a group. Since we started talking about human resources as a system, we have emphasized the team aspect. Teaching your staff to work together and report results together takes away individual threat and promotes cooperation.

We will start by looking at the recruiters' efficiency. How productive are their interviewing habits? What is the average length of interview for given types of jobs? How many interviews does it take to develop a list of qualified candidates? How many does it take to make a hire? Ratios for all these issues can be created. The most basic is average length of interview, as shown in Formula S–12.

Interview Time

$$AIL = \frac{h}{HI} \qquad (S-12)$$

where   AIL = average length of interviews*
    h = total hours spent interviewing (e.g., 6)
    HI = total number interviewed (e.g., 5)

EXAMPLE

$$AIL = \frac{6}{5}$$

$$AIL = 1.2 \text{ hours}$$

This can be accumulated for all recruiters and measured on a daily, weekly, or monthly basis and by exempt, non-exempt, or hourly job classification.

*AIL is computed by determining the total amount of time a recruiter spends interviewing divided by the total number of people interviewed.

This figure is needed as an input to other equations. It is a prerequisite to cost of hire measurement when staff time is involved, and it is necessary for measuring the cost of interviewing. It is also used in other indirect measures of recruiter efficiency and effectiveness.

Along with interviewing time, some staffing managers like to know how much time recruiters are spending on administrative duties. There is no clear definition of administrative time. Is it all activity other than application screening and interviewing? Does calling on sources of applicants, such as schools and nonprofit agencies, count as recruiting time or administrative time? I know managers who insist that their recruiters spend at least 15 percent of their time out of the office cultivating low-cost sources of applicants. Usually they consider this administrative time, but it is up to you to call it whatever you like. The point is that recruiters should be doing that kind of work and you may want to track it occasionally. A simple log kept by either the recruiter or the recruiter's assistant (clerk) will provide the data.

There is another efficiency measure which yields information about both your recruiters and your sources of applicants. It is called hire ratios. At first glance it looks very complicated. While it is complex in appearance it is quite simple to follow since there is a natural sequence to it. Formula S–13 lays it out.

Hire Ratios

$$HR = \frac{I}{A} \quad \frac{R}{I} \quad \frac{H}{R} \quad \frac{H}{A} \tag{S–13}$$

where   HR = hire rate
   A = applications received (e.g., 120)
   I = interviews (e.g., 30)
   R = referrals (e.g., 10)
   H = hires (e.g., 4)

EXAMPLE

$$HR = \frac{30}{120} \quad \frac{10}{30} \quad \frac{4}{10} \quad \frac{4}{120}$$
$$= 25\% \quad 33\% \quad 40\% \quad 3\%$$

Hire ratios trace the process from the point of application to the point of hire. It shows how the original pool of applicants is cut at each step. These computations can be made for all hires, or they can be done separately by source for different levels, job groups, or locations.

The first issue to look at is the ratio of applications to hires. Hypothetically, one could say that an advertisement which produced 120 applications was very effective. However, if you only obtained four hires, was it really effective? Consider the time, and therefore the cost, of processing those 120 applicants. Thirty got interviewed after someone plowed through 120 applications. Ten got a second interview by the line manager. That second interview might have been repeated by several other people in the requesting department as well. When the process was finally completed, with four hires, there was probably 50 to 60 hours of labor that went into it. Was that satisfactory?

I vividly recall the occasion when one of our field sales forces started a new sales training program. Without seeking advice from the staffing group they placed an ad and got over 300 responses. At that point we received a panicked cry for help. They only wanted to hire four people initially. As they plowed through the ever-growing stack of applications it was evident that anyone who had ever considered a sales career was applying. One might say that 300 applications was a great response. In fact, it was only a large response. The first screening eliminated over 280, and that was being generous. It took four people better than a day to accomplish the cut. That is not my idea of a productive ad.

The second issue that the hire ratio brings out is the efficiency of your recruiters' selection criteria. In the example, they screened 75 percent of the applications out, and after interviewing 30 people they referred 10 to management. Management selected four. That means that only 3 percent of the applicants actually got hired. None of these numbers has an intrinsic "rightness" or "wrongness." As you read the numerators, the denominators, and the percentages from left to right, you begin to get a feel for how the selection process is working. At first glance you may know how acceptable they are. Or, you may have to collect this data for a period of time until you can develop norms of acceptable practice. Either way, this measure can be a very helpful tool as part of your criteria for recruiting efficiency.

Another measure which tells us something about how productive your recruiters are is called the *hit rate* (HO). Simply stated, hit rate is the ratio of job offers made to job offers accepted, as shown in Formula S–14.

Hit Rate

$$HO = \frac{OA}{OE}$$ (S–14)

where   HO = percentage of offers which result in a hire
OA = offers accepted (e.g., 42)
OE = offers extended (e.g., 50)

EXAMPLE

$$HO = \frac{42}{50}$$

$$= 84\%$$

It is helpful to have an acceptable standard for this ratio. Under normal circumstances, you should be able to have perhaps three or four out of five offers accepted.

If a recruiter knows the client manager's idiosyncracies, comprehends the subleties of the requesting department, does a good job of screening and interviewing, and sees to it that the right salary and conditions are offered, it is not hard to reach at least a 75 percent hit rate. None of the criteria just mentioned are unreasonable. They are the knowledge and skills that a competent professional recruiter must have. The value of having a standard is that with a quick glance the staffing manager can tell how it is going. It will not be necessary to wait for someone to complain that you can't seem to hire people.

There is probably nothing more irritating, frustrating, and wasteful than an employment offer which is rejected. After your staff and the hiring department have spent many hours talking with candidates, checking references, comparing strengths and weaknesses, and preparing an offer it is very disheartening to be turned down. If it happens very often you will have a very unhappy clientele and a demoralized recruiting staff.

The value in tracking your hit rate is, as always, to generate a signal telling you that performance is unacceptable. When the signal flashes you can investigate and take steps to remedy the problem before your client senses it. For that reason it is important that your standards of performance be set higher than your client would demand. If, for example, your line managers feel that a 60 percent hit rate is acceptable, you will want to set your goal at 70 to 80 percent. This way you can drop to 65 percent, catch the signal, identify, and act on the problem before the rate drops to 60 percent. You always want to solve your problems before they become visible to the client. Your professional image depends on a high standard of performance.

QUANTIFYING THE QUALITATIVE

Up to this point we have been looking at ways to measure efficiency and productivity in the recruiting corps. In Chapter 2 we pointed out that effectiveness implies something beyond productivity. It embodies an expectation of desirability. It is not only doing something well; it is doing the important thing well. It is this issue of importance which brings in the subjective nature of quality and makes it more difficult to measure than productivity. The fundamental struggle in organizations has been between human resources people who see their work as purely qualitative, and management which wants some hard data to analyze. The key to closing this values gap depends on our ability to describe qualitative results with quantitative data.

For centuries, alchemists tried to turn lead into gold. They wanted to exchange the properties of one matter for that of another. Our job is much easier than that. We are not going to change anything; we are only trying to communicate a result through the medium of numbers rather than words.

Usually when people think about quantifying personnel work they look at the total function, which may encompass nearly 100 seemingly discrete tasks, and wonder how they can ever measure it. We have already demonstrated that the way to do that is to break down the function into those individual tasks which are in themselves quantifiable. That process of dividing a complex issue into identifiable parts is precisely the method we use to determine the quality of new hires. The only difference will be that we will build a quality measure not by defining tasks, but by selecting specific results which reflect the quality of the new employee.

Surely one of the most critical indices of a recruiter's effectiveness is the quality of the individuals who are hired. Recruiters may do many tasks well, but if they cannot come up with good candidates they must admit failure. The new hire is the end product of everyone's labor. The staffing manager, the recruiter, the clerical assistants, and the line manager are all involved in the process. Ultimately, the recruiter is the one who is held accountable for the quality of the end result.

The initial question is, how do we describe a good employee? Performance is the first indicator that comes to mind. Is that the only criterion? No. Promotability and stability also come into play. You may have others in mind to add to the list. For the sake of a simple example, I will work with these three. Recruiters deal with many applicants and generate many hires. In order to have a fair measure of the results of their labor, we should do a periodic evaluation of all hires. A semiannual review is a fair system to use for this purpose. There is usually enough activity in 6 months to smooth out any uncontrolled factors.

Patience is a prerequisite to measuring quality. We want to avoid flash-in-the-pan assessments. As you know, some new employees look great for the first few months, until they feel secure. After about 6 months the true nature of the individual becomes visible and evaluations made thereafter are normally more reliable.

Performance on the job, promotion to higher levels, and stability are all issues which cannot be measured for a minimum of 6 months. Only if an employee leaves in a short time can we assess stability. From a management standpoint, this may be disturbing. However, quality is inherently a long-term issue. Whenever we think about product quality we expect that the item will do not only what it is supposed to do, but that it will last. We have a right to expect a product to perform its function for a long time before we allow the manufacturer to proclaim its quality. Likewise, it is unreasonable to expect a qualitative assessment of a new employee in less than 6 months, and a full year is an even better appraisal period. With this as a basis of assumption, let us look at a quality of hire (QH) measure, as shown in Formula S–15.

Quality of Hire

$$QH = \frac{PR + HP + HS}{N} \qquad (S-15)$$

where   QH = quality of the people hired
   PR = average job performance ratings of new hires (e.g., 4 on a 5-point scale)
   HP = percent of new hires promoted within one year (e.g., 45%)
   HS = percent of new hires retained after 1 year (e.g., 90%)
   N = number of indicators used (e.g., 3)

EXAMPLE

$$QH = \frac{80 + 45 + 90}{3}$$
$$= \frac{215}{3}$$
$$= 71.7\%$$

The resulting percentage, 71.7 percent, is a relative value. It will be up to the person constructing the equation to decide if that number represents high, medium, or low quality. The decision can be based on historical comparison, preset performance standards or objectives, or management mandates.

Caution must be exercised in this matter. Performance ratings, promotions, and turnovers are all factors which are beyond the control of the recruiter. A good employee can be driven out by a poor supervisor, lack of promotional opportunity, job market conditions, and many other phenomena which have nothing to do with the recruiter. While this weakens the quality measure, it is no different than trying to assess the work of any employee. Even the most directly measureable professional performance can be unjustly damaged. Salespeople are adversely affected by recessionary markets and price cutting by competitors. Manufacturing managers can be hurt by obsolete equipment or lack of inventory. Business, no matter whether it is profit or not-for-profit, is an influenceable, not a controllable, activity. If you want to measure hire quality, this is the best known way of doing it. You must create a composite rating which includes several factors. The more controllable they are the better. But in any case the sum must be judged to be descriptive of a good employee. Because many of the components of effectiveness are largely uncontrollable, it is a measure which should not be widely broadcast outside the HR department. When used internally, the result must always be judged in the light of all mitigating circumstances known to the staffing manager.

Another less objective procedure for establishing a quality criterion is to ask the receiving department. You could ask the department to rate a new hire at the time of hire. Before the person goes to work, the receiving manager rates, and ranks if you like, this hire against all other hires during a given time period. The rating can be along a scale, say, 1 to 5 or 1 to 10. The ranking procedure is based on a comparison. A list would have to be maintained, and the receiver would insert the newest hire into the list in the appropriate slot. There are problems associated with establishing the validity of these types of opinions. Nevertheless, the measures are arrived at systematically, which implies some degree of reliability and objectivity.

RECRUITER EFFECTIVENESS

In order to answer the broader qualitative question of recruiter effectiveness, we will follow the same procedure used above but employ some different indices. The place to start is to ask, "what do recruiters do that makes the most difference?" Effective work is not performing one task, is it? It is the sum of many things done well. So, if we want to know how effective a recruiter is, we have to talk about several tasks. As an example, let us say that an effective recruiter sources, screens, recommends, and assists management in the hiring of good employees. Beyond that, effective recruiters respond quickly, fill jobs promptly, cut hire costs to a minimum, and maintain a high hit rate. Effective recruiters may do a few more things that make a difference, but for the sake of example let us stop there.

We have developed a list of important tasks which includes

* Response time
* Time to fill jobs
* Cost per hire
* Hit rate
* Quality of hires

When you do this you are free to select your own list. There is no mandatory group of tasks or results which add up to effectiveness in all situations. Qualitative terms are by nature open to subjective definition. All you need do is agree on the variables with the other people who are going to judge recruiter effectiveness. Assuming that you were to agree with my sample, the next step is to put them together so that they add up to effectiveness. We will follow the natural sequence of events so that the product will be a composite measure.

Recruiter Effectiveness

$$RE = \frac{RT + TF + HR + C/H + QH}{N} \qquad (S\text{--}16)$$

where　RE = overall recruiter effectiveness
RT = response time (e.g., 9 days)
TF = time to fill (e.g., 34 days)
HR = hire rate (e.g., 80%)
C/H = cost per hire (e.g., \$444)
QH = quality of hire (e.g., 71.7%)
N = number of indices used (e.g., 5)

You can decide to simply take the resulting numbers at face value and make a judgment of relative effectiveness. This is often sufficient, but if you want more objective data you can compare each number with a predetermined goal. If you perform the percent test on all indices, you will have converted the data to a common base. Then you can add all the percentages and divide by N to come out with a percentage of effectiveness, as shown in Fig. 6.4.

Proceed carefully in calculating percentage of goal achievement. In response time, goal is divided by result because the objective is to respond in 8 days or less. For time to fill and cost per hire, the objective is to fill in 45 days or less, at a cost of \$500 or less. In both cases this was achieved, so performance exceeded 100%. In quality of hire, result was divided by goal because the objective was to exceed 75%. The question of which is the divisor and which is the dividend depends on

Measure	Result	Goal	Goal achievement, weighted percentages
Response time	9 days	8 days	88 × 1.0 = 88
Time to fill	34 days	45 days	132 × 1.5 = 198
Hit rate	80%	80%	100 × 1.0 = 100
Cost per hire	$444	$500	113 × 2.0 = 226
Quality of hire	71.7%	75.0%	96 × 3.0 = 288
			900 ÷ 8.5 = 105.9

Figure 6.4   Recruiter Effectiveness

whether you want the result to be a higher or lower number than the goal.

If you believe that one measure is more important than another, you could weight the measures to correspond to your evaluation. You might say that time to fill is 1½ times more important than response time or hit rate. You might also say that cost per hire is two times and quality of hire is three times more important. Then you can multiply these factors times the percentages, add all five products, and divide by the sum of the weights. Mathematically, this is more proper than simply averaging unweighted percentages. Your result is a weighted evaluation of recruiter effectiveness. This is probably the most thorough computation you would consider. One step less would be to eliminate the weighting and simply compute an overall average percentage of effectiveness. The simplest procedure would be the first one, a face value check of the actual raw data, result.

Whichever method you choose, the fundamental principle is the same. Any subjective issue can be quantified by collecting and calculating data on several activities or results. Quality is an issue which requires more than one criterion, and it can be quantified.

Plan Ahead

FORECASTING PROBLEMS

The purpose of planning and forecasting is to increase an organization's options and to reduce the penalties incurred by inappropriate actions. The success of forecasting depends on the reliability of the data put into the system, the choice of models and methods used, and most importantly the linkage between the planners and forecasters and the line organization. In the best of all possible situations two conditions prevail. First, the planners are professionally competent and are respected for their ability to translate esoteric models and mountains of data into usable management information. Second, line management wants the planning system and will devote time to making it work. The business forecasts answer questions such as how many products or services will be sold monthly over the next 1 to 5 years. Human resources forecasting deals with the internal and external sources of people needed to make the business plan. The human resources plan profiles the existing work force, predicts the turnover rate, and projects the company's staffing needs by type, place, and time. Burack and Mathys[3] detail the factors, both internal and external, which impact forecasting. Internal factors affect the availability and utilization of personnel throughout the group, while external factors impact the recruitment of people. Figure 7.1 lists some of the variables in each category.

In all, there are over 25 inputs, any one of which can skew the results of a forecast. Despite the development of predictive techniques and

Internal	External
Budget restrictions	Competition
Production levels	Contract bidding
Sales/service levels	World trade
Organizational structure	External labor markets
Policy/manpower management allocations	Demographics
Internal labor market	Unions
Manpower planning competency	Education/skills
Contract services	Laws
Communications (openness of job info)	Economic climate
Organizational goals	Technology
Mergers or acquisitions	Work methods
Organizational climate	Equipment
Personnel programs	New products or services
Training	
Compensation	

Figure 7.1   Factors Affecting Forecasts

better sources of information, it is clear that forecasting is anything but a precise science. The future is still unknown and to a large extent unknowable. Stable industries and stable economic conditions increase our ability to predict. Nevertheless, for most organizations it appears that it will be some time yet before business plans are 99% accurate and perhaps longer still before management's human resources forecasts are reliable.

Because of this unpredictability, it is very difficult for the staffing manager to do planning for the staffing department itself. The issue is: given the uncertainty, how does a staffing department prepare itself to respond promptly to the demands made on it? Most companies will not allow staffing to carry excess employees. That is, you probably do not have the luxury of maintaining a 125 percent staff complement in order to be ready for any emergency. Since you have to try to operate with no more than the number of people you need at any given time, and because you know from experience that periodically you will be inundated with unplanned and unexpected recruiting demands—what can you do to mitigate the stress that will be put upon your staff while maintaining an acceptable level of recruiting support?

The answer to this question lies in selecting those variables which are most affected by changes in recruiting demand. The most common variables are your requisition inventory, the workload of your recruiters and their assistants (expressed in number of requisitions they are handling), the expected number of hires that can be attained by your recruiters and assistants in a given time period, and your past history of projected openings versus actual openings. These variables are influenced by your support systems and the nature of management's needs. If you redesign the work flow or automate, it should make a difference in the number of requisitions your staff can handle. If you choose to source through agencies versus advertising, it will impact your workload. If the ratio of exempt/non-exempt or professional/managerial requisitions changes, that may affect your response time and time to fill. Your ability to predict the future is dependent on your knowledge of the past, your perception of the present, and your skills in forecasting.

REQUISITION INVENTORIES

The first issue that the staffing manager needs to grasp is the size and variability of the requisition inventory. Requisitions are like orders: they come in, they are filled, and they go out. There are seasonal fluctuations in the requisition flow just like there are in the order flow. For instance, you know that more people quit their jobs and move during the summer. This causes the replacement requisition flow to increase. Some businesses, like food processing, hire to meet the need to harvest and process different crops. Retailers increase their staff for the Christmas season. Manufacturers of consumer goods direct their output to supplying different buying seasons. These cycles all dictate an uneven load of requisitions.

The staffing manager can predict with some amount of confidence that the cycles will repeat each year. Except when the economy is in a deep recession, the cycles will follow their normal patterns—only the amplitude will change. Staffing can track the number of requisitions opened each month and the level of requisitions at the beginning or end of each month. The measurement of this type of ebb and flow is accomplished by a simple addition process. A ratio may be used later when you compare time periods to each other or when you look at the number of new requisitions compared to the number filled or the number still in inventory. The three variations on this basic measure are shown in Formulas S–17 to S–19.

Requisitions Opened

$$RO = E_{RO} + SNE_{RO} + h_{RO} \qquad (S–17)$$

where RO = number of requisitions opened per month, by level

      E_{RO} = number of exempt requisitions opened (e.g., 35)

  SNE_{RO} = number of salaried non-exempt requisitions opened (e.g., 104)

      h_{RO} = number of hourly requisitions opened (e.g., 128)

EXAMPLE

$$RO = 35 + 104 + 128$$
$$= 267$$

In this example we tracked openings by level, but they could also be tracked by department, job group, or other criteria. This information could be recorded on a simple table or chart and updated each month. After 1 year the business cycle would be complete and cyclical fluctuations would be apparent. The next two measures would be calculated the same way.

Requisitions Filled

$$RF = E_{RF} + SNE_{RF} + h_{RF} \tag{S–18}$$

Requisition Inventory

$$RI = E_{RI} + SNE_{RI} + h_{RI} \tag{S–19}$$

These three indicators could be displayed on one table, as shown in Fig. 7.2. They could also be plotted on a trend chart and shown as three lines with months on the x axis and number on the y axis.

It is obvious that a manager of a staffing department needs to be able to predict the rate of incoming requisitions with some degree of accuracy. If there was no foreknowledge of the anticipated workload, it would be impossible to maintain a consistent level of service. One month the department might be overstaffed and the next woefully understaffed. If that were the pattern, the client organization, that is, line managers, would turn to outside sources to meet their recruitment needs.

Requisition flow is only part of the picture, however. The staffing managers also must know how efficient the recruiters are. In the previous chapter we discussed a few measures of efficiency and productivity —for example, length of interviews and hit rate. When we examined recruiter effectiveness we also discussed response time and time to fill. It is helpful as well to know how many requisitions a recruiter and the recruiting assistant can effectively handle; that is, how many requisitions they can work on in an efficient and effective manner. Observation of past performance will show, within a range of values, what the

Month	Opened			Filled			Remaining		
	E	SNE	h	E	SNE	h	E	SNE	h
Jan	35	104	128	21	95	126	14	9	2
Feb	41	109	136	35	107	131	20	11	7
Mar	43	101	95	52	104	100	9	8	2

Figure 7.2   Requisition Activity

optimum requisition load is for each recruiter and for the overall group. The manager also will want to have data on the hiring rates for different jobs. Some jobs are blessed with an overabundance of applicants. This is most often true for entry-level, blue-collar, and white-collar positions. Other jobs go begging because there are more openings than there are applicants. This is the case with several scientific and technical occupations. Because the total job market is characterized by such variability, the staffing manager cannot maintain an optimum work force without knowing the profile of the requisition load and the efficiency and productivity levels of the recruiting staff.

OPTIMIZING STAFF LEVELS

First we looked at the size or volume of the incoming workload, namely the flow of requisitions. Now we want to learn how the recruiting staff reacts to that flow. Obviously, people can handle as many as 100 requisitions if all they have to do is funnel resumes and applications to the requesting departments. However, if the job entails screening incoming paper, interviewing, checking references, and conferring with the requestor, then 100 requisitions is surely an unrealistic workload.

Since one of the notions underlying the term productivity is that the production is long term, let us use that as a working title for this question of optimum staff loading. The only way to arrive at an optimum factor is to track the hiring record of the recruiters and assistants over a long period of time. Seasonal fluctuations can distort short-term measures. As a minimum, I believe that you will have to have at least 6 months of production history before you can come to any conclusions. It is better to have the whole year to review, but if you do not have historical data and do not want to wait a year, then 6 months is a reasonable minimum.

The fundamental questions are, how many hires did the recruiters produce during each month? How many recruiters and how many assistants did you have on staff in each of those months? Putting those

Month	New hires	Number of recruiters	Average per recruiter	Number of assistants	Average per assistant
Jan	37	4	9.2	4	9.2
Feb	40	4	10	5	8
Mar	57	4	14.2	5	11.4
Apr	78	4	19.5	5	15.6
May	88	5	17.6	5	17.6
Jun	79	5	15.8	4	19.7
Jul	104	5	20.8	4	26
Aug	114	5	22.8	4	28.5
Sep	108	4	27	4	27
Oct	98	3	32.6	4	24.5
Nov	115	3	38.3	4	28.7
Dec	61	3	20.3	4	15.2
Averages		4	20.6	4.3	19.2
Total	979				
New hires planned	682				
Attrition*	370				
Needed for 1983	1052				

*Turnover projections predict 370 openings due to voluntary and involuntary terminations.

Figure 7.3   Staff Productivity Record

facts together you can come up with the average monthly number of hires per recruiter and per assistant. This is the basic measure, and a table as shown on Fig. 7.3 could be constructed.

This table shows the average number of hires per month throughout the reporting period. The optimum number is not necessarily the highest number. For example, November produced 38.3 hires per recruiter and 28.7 hires per assistant. This was the highest monthly average for both groups. However, issues of cost, quality, and customer service are also important for a department which is more than a paper funnel. The staffing manager will take several factors into consideration before deciding which months were the optimum service months. In this case the staffing manager reviews hire quality, cost per hire, and recruiter effectiveness measures and concludes that months 7 to 10 was the most effective recruiting period. During those months the recruiters generated an average of 25.8 new hires, while the assistants supported 26.5 hires. Since the projection is for 1052 open positions in 1983, the staffing manager divides that by 12 and finds an average of 87.7 openings per month. Dividing that number by the production record of the previous year, the manager finds a staffing level of 3.4 recruiters and 3.3 assistants.

This calculation is oversimplified, however, and it ignores the variability of the recruitment year. You know that there will be seasonal fluctuations of all types which will affect your requisition flow. You have a business plan for the organization which translates this into a projection of hiring needs. You probably have high and low periods of turnover which imply different levels of openings. All of these bits of information go into your estimate of new openings by month. Those 12 numbers would be the dividends and the hiring production record (i.e. 25.8) would be the divisor. This set of computations will give you a staffing level for each month throughout the coming year. By having people cross-trained, you can shift resources back and forth between functions and maintain an optimum level in your recruiting force.

As you track this recruitment function over a period of time you may find changes occurring which are not seasonal. General business conditions, such as a recession, usually help recruiters improve their time and cost factors because more people are writing in or coming in off the street looking for jobs. On the other hand, the arrival of a new company in town may create more competition for jobs and thereby make each hire more difficult. This adds time and money to the process and may also negatively impact the quality of hires due to scarcity of good labor. A staffing manager has to be aware of these unforeseen factors if an accurate staff level projection is desired.

ACTUAL VERSUS PROJECTED

I pointed out before that in order to project the future it helps to know the past. If Shakespeare was right and the past is prologue for what is to come, then we could use a convenient vehicle to record the past. The form which I propose illustrates the accuracy of the human resources planning system, as well as the organization's ability to accomplish its recruitment goals.

The form shown in Fig. 7.4 divides the data into two basic categories: additions to staff and replacements. Within those categories I have chosen to look at the data by the subdivisions of exempt, non-exempt, and hourly. As I have noted before, the subdivisions are a matter of personal choice. You may want to do it by occupations or by EEO categories. As always, it is up to you. The form provides space by category and subdivision to show the projected figure and the actual placement figure.

At the end of a reporting period, either monthly, quarterly, or annu-

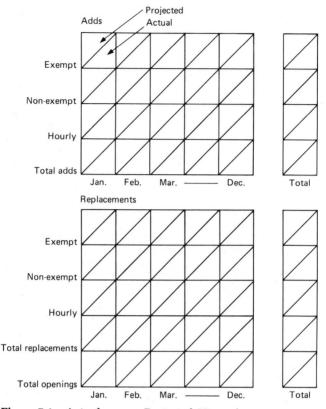

Figure 7.4   Actual versus Projected Hires

ally, you can check the correlation between the actual and the projected figures. Knowing how you have done by subdivision can help you strategize future recruitment efforts. For example, you may find that a given department, such as marketing, tends to project its needs either too high or too low. If this is a consistent pattern month after month, you might suspect that unless you can counsel them on projection techniques, you will have to inflate or deflate future projections by a certain amount. My experience is that people have levels of skill and optimism which lead them to be a little high or a little low. Furthermore, this does not seem to change without some intervening event, such as training. Therefore, according to my experience as staffing manager, I could take the annual projections and inflate some while deflating others. The result was that my actual came closer to my projected than it had before I bothered to study the patterns and make adjustments. This helped me plan my staffing levels more accurately. And whenever a new player got into the game I would start my observations over again.

The most successful people I know all exhibit the habit of planning. It seems that they always have the time to study and plan before they act. On the other hand, the people who I would classify as moderately successful to unsuccessful seem to spend more time acting and less time planning. They are the personification of the notion that they do not have time to plan, but they do have time to do it over when it goes wrong. Perhaps there is a lesson to be learned from these two approaches.

SUMMARY

We have looked at the staffing function and measured it with the four basic indices: cost, time, quality, and quantity. The examples given were not meant to be all-encompassing. Rather, they were samples of what I consider, based on over 6 years of operating a measurement system, to be the most important tasks to measure. I do not suggest that you use all the sample formulas. Instead, you should choose a few that have particular value for your situation. Furthermore, you should feel free to modify the sample to fit your needs. The way these formulas are expressed is not the only acceptable form. Consider your environment, your staff, line management, business conditions, organizational objectives, and anything else which may impact the staffing function. Then design a set of measures and reports which will help you meet the twin goals of effective management and persuasive reporting.

SECTION

C

HOW TO MEASURE
COMPENSATION
AND BENEFITS

The Wage and Salary System

THE MOST POPULAR TOPIC

Compensation is the one subject within the personnel administration sphere that everyone wants to talk about. It is often difficult to involve managers and supervisors in studies of planning, training, recruitment, or employee relations programs. But let it be known that you are going to review and revise the compensation system and you will find people knocking down your door to be on the project team. This is quite reasonable. Everybody, no matter how smart or stupid they are, understands two factors in life: pain and pleasure. They view their pay as either one or the other. Most of us can always use more money, and when someone brings up the subject we are always anxious to talk about it. We want to lobby for a bigger share of the pie or, in the worst case, protect what we have. The challenge for the compensation manager is not to get people interested, it is to convince them that the system is equitable and they should use it rather than subvert it.

If you ask yourself how you know if your compensation program is doing its job, what would be your answer? The answer to that is, of course, "it depends." What does it depend on? It depends on what it is supposed to be doing. So, what is the purpose of the compensation system? Whenever I ask that question the reply is usually something like, "compensation's mission is to assist in attracting, retaining, and motivating employees." That answer is two-thirds right. Technically, motivation is an inherent trait of human beings. You cannot motivate a person; you can only stimulate or incent employees. It is a small point, but for the sake of precision and education of managers, I believe it is worth noting. The implication of incent versus motivate is profound when applied to managing people. However, this is not the place to go into it in depth. In this case, we need only the notion that motivation is internal and incentive is external.

COMPLEXITY

Designing compensation programs is a complex process. There is much more to it than doing a salary survey and spreading some numbers across a form. The compensation department must understand the processes for planning, projecting, and administering. It must also be comfortable with statistical procedures. In addition, it needs to be able to synthesize data from many sources and shape it into a structure that everyone can understand and use. That structure must be able to meet the reasonable needs and demands of employees, as well as mesh with the philosophy of the organization and its ability to pay. All of this cannot be attained through haphazard methods. It requires the development of a system. History has shown time after time that organizations must systematize their compensation function. The inevitable consequences of the laissez-faire approach have been rampant inequities, poor morale, productivity breakdowns, and increased turnover. As I pointed out before, people understand the value of money in their lives. They will put up with a lot of managerial ineptitude except when it comes to pay.

Since it is clear that a system is required, can we identify and therefore measure the components of the system? By tracing the processes indigenous to a compensation system and the results which the system yields we can find things to measure. The potential trap lies in measuring the usage and outcomes of the system and implying that this equates with the productivity or effectiveness of the compensation department. In some sense it does and in another it does not. The point is important, and the issue is complex enough that we need to spend time now clearly establishing the rationale for our different measurement criteria.

First, referring to our definitions of productivity and effectiveness, you recall we said that productivity relates to levels of performance in valued activities. Effectiveness is doing the right thing—getting the desired result. The two issues are semantically discrete but pragmatically inseparable. It is hard to imagine effective performance which is carried out in an unproductive fashion. Nevertheless, I will offer a way of looking at the compensation department from both a productive and an effective viewpoint.

The compensation department attempts to fulfill its organizational role of assisting in attracting, retaining, and incenting employees by focusing on the following. First, it builds and maintains a system of performance appraisal and pay. Second, it controls the cost of the pay program not just by monitoring the dollar cost, but also by influencing the way in which supervisors and managers exercise the program. The third point is a result of the first two. The compensation staff tries to communicate the pay and performance appraisal system to the employees so that they will understand how and why it works the way it does. Additionally, the compensation department strives to convince employees, by monitoring management pay practices, that the system is just, equitable, and competitive.

The way to judge the compensation department's productivity or effectiveness is to look at each of the focal activities separately, starting with administration. Once the system is designed it must be maintained. Maintenance is more of an efficiency or productivity question than an effectiveness question. The pay system is composed of components and processes. Job descriptions, job evaluation, compa-ratios (which describe the movement of salaries compared to the midpoint of the range), and such are the building blocks of a pay structure. They have to be cared for. Performance objectives can be set for maintenance tasks and the results measured. These are issues internal to the department and subject to measures of efficiency and productivity.

Cost control is an activity of the compensation department. However, the results of that activity are external to the department. Costs are, to be sure, a function of the way system components are handled. For example, writing job descriptions and leveling jobs impacts salary expenses. You can measure productivity by calculating how long it took the compensation analyst to write a job description (JD) or level a group of jobs. However, you measure the effectiveness of the work by what happens when managers use those descriptions and salary grades. The work is effectively done if managers can attract, retain, and incent people and still stay within the salary budget. By definition, if a system meets its objectives and does so with an acceptable level of employee satisfaction, it is effective. The second part of that definition leads us to the third focal point of measurement in compensation.

Employee satisfaction is a phenomenon totally external to the compensation department, yet it is dependent in part on the work of the compensation staff. There are a number of vehicles available to the department for explaining their system to employees. The most direct methods are meetings and written communiques. However, the one that counts above all others is the manner in which an individual's supervisor utilizes the system. The role of the compensation manager is to make sure that line managers are handling the system in the manner intended. The best way to determine that is through employee surveys and exit interviews. When it comes to pay questions, people are seldom reticent to tell you what they think and feel. A less formal but easily accessible source of effectiveness data is daily feedback. Your staff usually knows how people feel about their pay. They hear about it all the time if they are maintaining good contacts with the employees as a whole. If employees understand and feel good about the pay program, it is fair to claim that your staff has done an effective job.

In summary, it is relatively easy to measure your compensation staff's productivity. Primarily, it requires a judgment of how efficiently they are carrying out their tasks. Several examples will be presented in this chapter. Effectiveness, since it is a subjective term, is more ambiguous. In order to have a good measure of effectiveness, it is necessary to create a composite consisting of several external, outcome variables. In Chapter 6 we did that to judge recruiter effectiveness. While composites are not as neat as a single unequivocal measure, they are the best and only way to generate a defensible indicator.

SYSTEM MAINTENANCE

Salary structures usually start with the development of job descriptions. Following closely on job descriptions is the job evaluation and leveling process. The result of the interaction between the description and leveling processes is a salary structure. One of the truest statements about structures is that they cannot stand still, but instead must be dynamic. The structure must be reviewed at least annually. In cases where jobs are plentiful and people are moving frequently, some part of the salary structure must be constantly under review. In that sense, salaries are like big bridges: they need constant touchups. The Golden Gate and the Veranzano Narrows bridges are so large that the painting crews never stop scraping, sanding, and painting them. By the time they get to one end it is time to start repainting at the other.

The components which hold a salary structure together must be periodically examined also. Since jobs change, job descriptions have to be rewritten. The proactive manager sets goals for auditing job descriptions, and the achievement of those goals can be quantified, as shown in Formula C–1.

Job Description Factor

$$JDF = \frac{JD}{J} \qquad\qquad (C\text{–}1)$$

where JDF = percent of jobs having formal, current job descriptions

JD = number of jobs with current descriptions (e.g., 312)

J = total number of jobs in the system (e.g., 339)

EXAMPLE

$$JDF = \frac{312}{339}$$
$$= 92\%$$

Auditing the job description is just part of the task. It helps recruiters who need up-to-date information to fill jobs. However, unless it is followed by job evaluation and leveling, the salary structure does not benefit. Thus, system maintenance is a two-step process. Once job descriptions are rewritten, then job evaluations are conducted and the structure is releveled. Just as maintenance goals are set for descriptions, so should they be set for evaluation and leveling. Formula C–2 gives the job evaluation factor.

Job Evaluation Factor

$$JEF = \frac{JE}{J} \tag{C–2}$$

where JEF = percent of jobs which have been evaluated and leveled

JE = number of jobs evaluated and leveled (e.g., 308)

J = total number of jobs in the system (e.g., 339)

EXAMPLE

$$JEF = \frac{308}{339}$$
$$= 91\%$$

Another way of looking at the vitality of the system is to approach it from an exception standpoint. How many exceptions exist within the structure, or how often do we have to make adjustments in order to achieve a worthwhile objective? Two examples of this are salary range exceptions, commonly referred to as "red circles," and salary adjustments usually made for a group of jobs.

In the first case it is worthwhile to know what percent of your employees have salaries which exceed the maximum for their grade. The calculation is simple, as shown in Formula C–3.

Salary Range Exception Factor

$$SO = \frac{RC}{e} \qquad (C\text{--}3)$$

where SO = percent of employees over salary grade maximums
       RC = number of red circles (e.g., 3)
        e = average number of employees (e.g., 71)

EXAMPLE

$$SO = \frac{3}{71}$$
$$= 4.2\%$$

Red circles are indicators of abnormalities. They may show that there is an aging and stagnant employee population. For whatever reasons, a number of people may have "maxed out" and are not able to move up to the next higher grade. Besides being a structural problem it also creates an abnormally high labor cost. An organization may not be able to tolerate many salaries above the maximum for the range. Another question that red circles, or the request to red circle someone, may bring out is poor salary management. Managers sometimes use salary dollars to try to solve interpersonal problems. For example, they may have employees who should be counseled about lack of effort to qualify themselves for promotion. Instead of facing the issue, the manager requests a salary increase above range maximum. Keeping track of the red circle brigade is one means of monitoring the system, which also pays off by pointing out organizational or managerial problems.

A second example of exceptions has to do with requests for salary adjustments. Periodically market conditions change and cause organizations to adjust their salary ranges. Usually this occurs on a semiannual or annual basis. It is the normal, scheduled way that structures get updated. However, it may happen that some unforeseen market perturbation takes place and forces an unplanned adjustment in a specific job family. Take the case where we suddenly learn that a competitor is now paying programmers 15 percent more than we are. We can choose to hold the line, and predictably it will be more difficult to recruit programmers. We may also begin to experience high turnover in that group as they learn what is being offered elsewhere. More often than not we will choose to adjust the salary range and the salaries of our current programming staff.

That kind of a situation can and does come up in every organization from time to time. However, if we find that it seems to be happening with great frequency, it might signal the need to audit the structure.

It sometimes happens that we forego a semiannual or annual adjustment to the structure because we believe that we can safely go another 6 months without moving the ranges. Then we begin to experience a rather constant stream of requests to make adjustments. In this case we have miscalculated or ignored information that might have predicted the need to adjust. Adjustments for a specific group may have an unsettling effect on the larger organization. If another group hears about it, and they always will, they begin to look for reasons why they, too, deserve an unscheduled raise. Soon a ripple spreads out across the organization, and the compensation department finds itself under severe pressure to meet both supportable as well as insupportable demands. In such cases, the management of the system has been taken away from the department.

There is no need to create a formula to track the frequency of adjustments. The point is to note that adjustments are exceptions to a system, and if there are too many exceptions this implies that the system is no longer functional.

OPERATING GOALS

For a measure to have meaning there must be a standard against which it can be compared. This basic premise holds for all applications, including those in compensation. I do not believe that it is sufficient to simply report on the pay system in terms of how much money has been spent. Cost is the result of the operation of the system, not a cause. By focusing on the internal workings of the system you will be able to affect cost, not merely observe and react to it.

Within the structure itself we can set checkpoints which tell us that the system has reached a certain point of maturity. An example of this is a *compa-ratio target,* the calculation of which results in a percentage figure which tells us whether or not the actual salaries in a given pay grade are higher or lower than the midpoint, on the average. We can establish the standard that when a compa-ratio exceeds a certain percentage we will automatically review these salaries and that part of the salary range structure. In effect, this standard becomes a trigger point which automatically sets off a review. The calculation is quite simple. Establish your trigger point, e.g., 110 percent. This point is reached when the average salary in a job group exceeds the midpoint of the pay range by 10 percent. An example would be

$$\text{Average salary} = \$22,000$$
$$\text{Midpoint} = \$20,000$$
$$\text{Compa-ratio} = 110\%$$

Goals can also be established for the use of the system. Performance appraisals and salary increases are the processes by which management gives expression to a compensation system. Some companies have set standards in both processes. The standards are used to control the expenditure of salary dollars and to induce supervisors and managers to give some thought to the way they handle performance appraisals. It is at this point that the line between maintenance and cost control becomes blurred.

COST CONTROL

Periodically, all employees are entitled to a review of their performance. In a study of organizational communications interest, it was found that employees were much more interested in performance and career opportunity information than in any other topic. There has probably been as much research and speculation on performance reviews and appraisals as on any managerial subject. Operating philosophies have been created to inform and support managers so that they can do a more credible, constructive job. Elaborate procedures have been developed to help managers review their employees, management by objectives being the best example of that approach. And yet, even with all this very few companies are happy with their review systems.

As a last resort some organizations have gone to setting up a standard profile by which they expect managers to distribute the performance appraisals in their group. Some insist on using the bell-shaped curve. With it they say, in effect, most issues, activities, and outcomes are naturally distributed on the curve. Therefore, we will expect that the performance scores you give your group will be more or less normally distributed. That is, a very small percentage will receive the highest possible rating; a slightly larger number will receive the next highest rating; most of the people will be about in the middle; and the remainder will be spread down the backside of the curve. Management may sometimes become very specific and say that no more than 10 percent can receive the top rating, the second level should include about 20 percent, 40 percent should set a middle rating, 20 percent a low one, and 10 percent should probably be on probation.

Whether or not your organization explicitly states a preferred or desired distribution of appraisal scores, you can track what the actual results have been. There is a value in seeing the distribution pattern. I have found that by working with organizations to set a desired distribution, tracking the actual pattern, and reporting it to them, peer pres-

Division	Number of employees	Performance level 5		Performance level 4		Performance level 3		Performance level 2		Performance level 1	
		#	%	#	%	#	%	#	%	#	%
A	885	15	1.7	566	64.0	231	26.1	71	8.0	2	0.2
B	565	42	7.4	329	58.2	168	29.7	26	4.6	0	0
C	590	38	6.4	220	37.3	272	46.1	60	10.2	0	0
D	260	20	7.7	113	43.5	95	36.5	32	12.3	1	0.3
E	178	22	12.4	110	61.8	38	21.3	8	4.5	0	0
F	134	24	17.6	86	64.7	20	14.7	4	3.0	0	0
Corporate total	2612	161	6.2	1424	54.5	824	31.5	201	7.8	3	0.1

Figure 8.1   Performance Appraisal Distribution

sure could serve as the monitoring mechanism. Once all parties agree to a pattern, if one slips significantly above or below it, the peer group forces the culprit back in line. This approach has two advantages. First, it takes the compensation manager out of the confronting or adversary role. Second, the system achieves what it was set up to do: reward performance and control costs.

One way to display the distribution data for several groups is to put it on a table. On the y axis, or side, list the departments and the number of employees. On the x axis, along the top, place the performance levels so that they are column headings. It is helpful to show both the number of people appraised at a particular level and the percent of the whole which that represents. Figure 8.1 is a sample performance appraisal table.

It is relatively easy to see both how each department did against the goal and how they compared to each other. Was one consistently high? Was another consistently low? Either way, if the differences are significant they can act as precursors of organizational problems.

A quicker evaluation can be made if you plot those percentages as curves on a graph. If you have color graphic capability, five or six groups can be shown on the same chart without confusion. If you have set a desired distribution curve, you can also plot that. Then everyone can quickly see the correlations and deviations between the standard and the actual.

Salary increase patterns can be handled in the same manner. Many organizations set increase standards; for example, they may decide that the average increase should be 9 percent in the coming year. Within that parameter, they may allow managers to distribute increases as they see fit. Other organizations may structure the process by dictating minimum and maximum increases throughout the system.

No matter which way the system is set up the results can be displayed to show how they compare to the standards. The principle is the same for salary increase displays as it was for performance appraisals. When using a tabular format the vertical axis shows the departments, set in a column along the left side. The elements to be reviewed are placed across the top as column headings. For example, the columns may be levels—i.e., hourly, non-exempt, and exempt—or job groups— i.e., programmers, engineers, accountants, and secretaries. The average salary increase percentage is then recorded in the appropriate position on the table.

Increase patterns can also be shown in a bar chart format. The percentage increase is placed on the vertical y axis from 0 up to a maximum of your choice. The groups to be viewed are arranged across the horizontal x axis. Be aware that the larger the y scale, the less the differences between groups will appear to be. For instance, on a standard 8½ X 11 sheet a percentage range of 20 points will make the differences between measured groups smaller than a range of 15 points. A wide range lessens the visual impact. So, if your maximum recorded increase is 14 percent, use a 15-percent scale. The difference between the lengths of bars will be more dramatic than if you use a 20-percent scale. Always keep in mind the fact that a report is supposed to both inform and to make a point. So, construct a chart which tells your story as effectively as possible.

Another goal-type measure is quite common and most organizations have it: the salary budget. Budgets are constructed from different perspectives but they all end up at the same point—they tell managers how many total dollars can be spent on salaries. Most budget systems kick out a monthly or quarterly report which shows the variance between actual and budgeted figures. If you do not have such a system, it is relatively easy to do the calculation yourself. Somewhere in the accounting system the salary account is subtotaled by department and then totaled for the whole organization. Simply divide those numbers by the budgeted figure and see what the variance is. If you do it on a month-to-month basis, you can see loosening or tightening trends across a range of departments. Your results can be reported in either dollar or percentage variance.

DISTRIBUTION PATTERNS

The last section, where we looked at increase patterns, is a precursor to a discussion of distribution patterns. The underlying issue in both is, how are managers using the system? I pointed out earlier that we cannot design systems and then disavow the way they are used. I believe that our job is to guide management in the proper utilization of the programs we develop. This is not always easy, as you know from experience. Nevertheless, it is our obligation to not only design the vehicle and train people how to drive it, but also monitor their driving habits and point out faults and hazards as we see them. This is where the concept of effectiveness comes in. Just as bad driving habits are dangerous to the safety of driver, occupants, and bystanders, so inappropriate and improper use of a salary program can be unfair to employees and dangerous for the organization. When pay is distributed incorrectly, some employees will benefit while others suffer. Furthermore, the organization is jeopardized. Poor pay practices usually lead to higher turnover, lower morale, and in some cases legal actions against the organization. There have been many cases over the past decades where class-action suits have resulted in multimillion dollar backpay awards. And for every case that makes it to court, there are undoubtedly dozens which are settled quietly and privately.

Compensation managers have a mechanism which they can use to study the distribution of individual salaries within a salary grade. If a salary structure is set up so that there are four subdivisions to each salary grade, it is called a *quartile structure.* The method that is used to calculate the distribution pattern reveals how many people have a salary within each quartile of a given grade. When those figures are plotted, it is called a *maturity curve.* From a technical standpoint this is a very valuable measure for the compensation department. It tells them how well their structure is aging. That is, are there too many people high in the grade? That would mean that the structure probably needs to be adjusted. It could also mean that the employee population is stagnating and an excessive number of people are "topping out," which is an organizational issue as well as a compensation problem.

We want to look at salary distribution from an equity point of view. We must make sure that there is no case of intentional or unintentional discrimination. There are at least two ways of doing this. The more precise method is to use a variation of the maturity curve calculation described above. In this case we would look at salary distribution across quartiles of each grade for each of the groups we wanted to examine. For EEO purposes, we would do it for each affected category. Obviously,

Salary grade	EEO category							Others
	B	H	O	I	F	A	H	
10	980	978	1018	950	985	1040	964	1000
20	1085	1077	1139	1078	1085	1159	1090	1110
30	1235	1237	1270	1238	1356	1301	1229	1280

Figure 8.2   Patterns of Average Monthly Salaries by Employee Group

this is a very complex and time-consuming calculation, which cannot be performed easily without computer assistance. If you choose to do it, you have to construct a separate table for each category. You would probably set up the table with salary grades in the first column. Quartiles 1 to 4 would constitute the next 4 columns. Each quartile position on the table would display either the number of people or the percentage of people from that category whose salary fell into that position. For you to know whether or not the resulting distribution profile were discriminatory, you would have to do the same thing for the non-affected categories of employees. I am certain that you can appreciate the magnitude of the task.

A simpler way to obtain a sense of whether or not you had a problem would be to use average salaries for each group, as shown in Fig. 8.2. By using an average you eliminate the task of spreading individual salaries across a grade. This approach also allows you to display data on all categories on one page. When the table is filled in you can scan it for any obvious or serious disparities. This is the simplest way of doing the job, though you could convert actual salaries into percentiles. I do not see the value of going to the extra labor, however. Many people have difficulty dealing with percentiles, and actual average salaries don't really need any interpretation.

There is a hidden danger in dealing with averages. Averages lump together all salaries and in the process ignore the differences among them. As a result, the average may look fine, but you may have within that a few people who are a long way from the mean. For example, look at these two cases on page 115.

In case 1 there is only about a 10-percent variance to either side of Mary's salary, which happens to fall right on the mean. There is probably no cause for alarm or claim of unfair treatment. However, in case 2 there is nearly a 40-percent variance to either side of Mary. Furthermore, Lee is making less than half of what John makes. By using averages we never know what pitfalls may lie within.

The way to eliminate the problem with averages is to calculate

Case 1		Case 2	
John's salary	$1000	John's salary	$1500
Mary's salary	1100	Mary's salary	1100
Lee's salary	1200	Lee's salary	700
Average salary	1100	Average salary	1100

standard deviations for each average. A standard deviation tells you how wide a spread there is between individual salaries and the average salary. In the two cases we looked at, while the average salary was exactly the same, the standard deviations were vastly different. It is a simple matter to program a computer to do standard deviations, and even many handheld calculators are capable of doing them.

Distribution studies can be made for a variety of issues. Besides affected categories you could look at pay patterns across departments, locations, or any other classification which you had a hunch might be hiding or breeding a problem. Compensation managers are responsible for monitoring the system that they design. They owe it to their organizations to be a watchdog on issues of pay. Conducting a distribution study once a year goes a long way toward ensuring that no one can ever bring a successful class-action pay suit against you.

COST ANALYSIS

In most organizations the payroll costs are the largest or the second largest single expense item. The two most common calculations are total cost of payroll and average salary cost per employee. There is no mystery to the whys and hows of these. However, there are some other variations on these basic measures which are useful.

An often overlooked cost item is payroll taxes. An organization not only pays its employees an hourly rate or a monthly salary, it also pays a significant amount of money to the government. These funds go for social security, income taxes, unemployment insurance, and in some states disability insurance. To appreciate how much this could amount to, you can compute a payroll tax factor, as shown in Formula C–4.

Payroll Tax Factor

$$\text{PTF} = \frac{\text{PT}}{\text{C}} \qquad \text{(C–4)}$$

where   PTF =   portion of total salary or wages (including bonus and incentive pay) absorbed by payroll taxes

PT =   sum of payroll tax deductions for social security (FICA), federal and state income taxes, unemployment insurance, and state disability where applicable (figures will vary by state and by income level)

C =   Total compensation (i.e., salary, bonus and/or commission)

EXAMPLE

$$PTF = \frac{FICA + FIT + SIT + UI + SDI}{\text{Salary/wages (+ bonus and incentives)}}$$

Both the magnitude and the rate of growth of this expense item are becoming critical operating concerns for management. I believe that compensation departments should keep these numbers in front of management. The executives who run organizations owe it to their stockholders and employees to be cognizant of this cost and to be active in dealing with the various governmental bodies to see that it does not get out of hand.

Some industries have kept track of the relationship of the number of employees and the cost of compensation as they relate to other operating variables. The change in the rate of growth of employees or compensation expense has been compared to rates of change for gross revenues and expenses, operating and net income, or the other input costs of capital, energy, material, and plant. These variables are basics of a business whether it be profit or not-for-profit. One matchup that many firms have been interested in is employees and revenues. By dividing total revenue by total employees they obtained a number which they could track as one mark of efficiency. If revenues equalled $100 million and there were 2000 employees, the ratio would be $50,000 per employee. If this number improved significantly, it was a sign that effectiveness was increasing. The improvement was not necessarily all in factory productivity. It might have been that salespeople were becoming more efficient or that engineering had simplified a design or that manufacturing had automated a procedure. The reason was not necessarily obvious, but the result was clearly positive. Of course, a decrease in the number would indicate a deterioration in performance somewhere.

A similar efficiency measure is the average hourly rate. It is calculated as shown in Formula C–5.

Average Hourly Rate

$$R/h = \frac{P}{EHW} \qquad (C\text{-}5)$$

where   R/h = average hourly wage or salary paid
          P = total wages and salaries paid (e.g., $57,017,000)
       EHW = Total employee hours worked, number of hours times number of employees (e.g., 35,000 X 174)

EXAMPLE

$$R/h = \frac{\$57,017,000}{35,000 \times 174}$$
$$= \frac{\$57,017,000}{6,090,000}$$
$$= \$9.36$$

By adding the hours worked element we have refined a gross compensation number into an hourly one. This is more workable. It is difficult for a person to deal with an eight-digit number. The figure $57,017,000 is useful to rally support for an efficiency or productivity drive, but $9.00 is a human scale number. Employees can say to themselves, "If I can find a way to save just 10 cents an hour, that will save the company over a half million dollars!" Most people can think of ways to save a dime, but they do not deal with $500,000 often enough to know where to start.

We have looked at cost from several perspectives. The last one was from the cost of function. The work force can be divided into many groups, such as level, job group, department, and location. One other function is supervision and management. Few people consider what it costs an organization to manage itself. Consider the proportion of your organization which is populated by supervisors and managers. This category includes everyone from first line supervisor to chief executive officer. All of these people exist in the organization, yet they are not producers. Their job is to manage the work of others. The question is, how much does it cost you for that service? The simplest way to find out is to compute a cost to supervise factor.

Cost to Supervise

$$SC = \frac{TSS}{TS} \qquad (C\text{-}6)$$

	Current organization	Proposed organization
1. Total employees	_____	_____
2. Number of exempt	_____	_____
3. Number of non-exempt	_____	_____
4. Number of supervisors	_____	_____
5. Total salary dollars paid to unit	_____	_____
6. Total salary dollars paid to supervisors	_____	_____
7. Total exempt salary dollars	_____	_____
8. Total non-exempt salary dollars	_____	_____

Definitions

Employees — All full-time and part-time employees expressed as average number and personnel reporting to the unit including the unit head.

Exempt — All employees of grade_____ and above.

Non-exempt — All employees of grade _____ and below.

Supervisor — Any supervisor/manager with direct reporting responsibility for one or more subordinates.

Unit — Organizational department or subgroups.

Figure 8.3   Staffing Measures Worksheet

where   SC = supervision cost

TSS = total salaries paid to supervisors (e.g., $315,900)

TS = total salaries paid (e.g., $1,727,700)

EXAMPLE

$$SC = \frac{\$315,900}{\$1,727,700}$$

$$= 18.3\%$$

This type of measure can be useful when considering the reorganization of a work group. The Occidental Consulting Group has developed a procedure for evaluating the cost impact of a reorganization using this method. One of the forms they use is shown in Fig. 8.3.*

Beyond all that we have talked about there are still some questions that compensation might be able to address. Remember, we made a case early on for the interrelated nature of human resources functions. By

*Used by permission.

looking at hiring and employee relations issues we can find evidence of compensation program effectiveness. Where there is effect we might be able to identify cause. Here are a couple of questions that could be asked of other human resources sections:

1. Are we able to consistently hire below midpoint? The answer to this tells us if our structures are staying competitive. New hire records will show starting salaries.

2. Are people leaving for the same level job and getting substantially more money? This is another approach to the competitive structure question. The answer to this one can be found in exit interviews.

3. If there are incentive programs, such as piece rates and bonuses, do the people feel that they are challenging and fair? Surveys and interviews will provide the answers to this question.

4. Do supervisors and managers find the system easy to understand and, more importantly, explain to their staffs? Again, surveys and interviews will tell the story.

There are many more questions like these that can be asked about the system. In every case answers are available. When these are put into the mix with the more quantitative issues, a well-rounded evaluation of the compensation function emerges.

EMPLOYEE PAY ATTITUDES

Entirely outside of the pay system and its utilization is the reaction of employees to their pay. Since our behavior is largely based on our perceptions of our environment, and since pay is part of our perceptual field, it follows that employees' view of their pay must correlate with some aspects of work behavior. What is not yet proved is exactly how, when, and how much attitudes impact behavior on the job. If you want your compensation department to be effective in terms of optimizing the organization's return on its salary dollars, pay attitudes have to be addressed. Lawler[1] has reviewed the research on the importance of pay and concludes

Most of the research is fragmented, noncumulative, and poorly designed. Most of the forty-nine studies [reviewed by Lawler] that have tried to determine how important pay is represent a great expenditure of effort that contributes virtually nothing to our understanding. By selectively using the data from these studies, one can argue any position . . .

Smith and Wakeley[2] pointed out that pay has been viewed from several standpoints by theorists

1. Money is a general means to satisfying needs.
2. Money is a basic incentive.
3. Money may be an anxiety reducer.
4. Money keeps workers from being dissatisfied but does not motivate.
5. Money is an instrument to attaining a valued goal.

No matter which view you subscribe to, you would probably agree that pay is an important issue in the minds of your work force.

I believe that people fundamentally ask themselves two questions about their pay. First, am I paid fairly? Is the amount of money I make appropriate for the effort and responsibility I put into the job? Second, does the ratio of my input to my outcome compare favorably with the same ratio for other workers in my company, locale, and industry?

Since pay is important to your employees, you will want to know as much about their attitudes toward your system and its utilization as you can. The most common way of obtaining that information is through interviews and surveys. Structured and unstructured interviews at orientation, during a person's employment, or at the time of termination can elicit a good deal of useful information. Surveys are much more complicated and time-consuming. They also can cause more harm than good if they are not administered properly. There are many surveys available commercially. Some offer extensive computer-based analysis as well as national and regional norms. It is not the purpose of this chapter to review them. My objective in mentioning surveys is simply to point out that they are probably necessary in some form if you want to find out how effective your pay program is in the eyes of the recipients. Also, I want to caution those who have not used surveys extensively that they are not as straightforward as they appear. I firmly believe that surveys should never be conducted with large groups of employees without professional assistance. My observation is that a very significant percentage of surveys backfire on the user due to lack of knowledge on how to design or conduct them, rash judgment of the results, or inappropriate or nonexistent followup with those surveyed. My conclusion is that it is important to know how your employees perceive their pay, and the only way to obtain that perception is through some formal structured interview or survey. However, be careful how you go about it. Pay may or may not be the most important issue on the minds of employees, but there are few issues that are more sensitive.

SUMMARY

Although the compensation function deals mainly with quantitative issues, there are relatively few measures of efficiency and productivity. Staffing lends itself more to that type of evaluation because it is basically project work. Each opening is like a project, with a beginning and an end, whereas compensation is more like a process. It is a continuous flow with few clear checkpoints. It is very difficult to determine undeniable cause and effect relationships. Compensation has maintenance tasks whose efficient accomplishment can be evaluated. However, the results are of interest only to the compensation and human resources management.

In order to grasp the full value of the compensation function we have to study it more from an effectiveness perspective. Many different indices are gathered and viewed as a composite picture. In the end we make a judgment that goes something like this. The compensation system has a purpose which is quite far-reaching, important, and complex. To achieve its mission it must establish and maintain a structure, and we can audit whether or not it is attending to that responsibility. The second task for compensation is to service the needs of the organization with a minimum of exceptions to the system. We can track system utilization to see how well it is operating against preset standards and goals. Since creation of pay equity is a fundamental mission, we can look at the results of the use of the system to determine if pay is being properly distributed across all groups. We can also measure the cost of wages and salaries and check to see if it is within acceptable ranges. Finally, we can measure employee attitudes toward the pay and performance appraisal system.

By evaluating how well the organization is doing across this wide range of indices, we can make a judgment as to the effectiveness of the compensation department. What is difficult to do is to point out how the function makes a direct impact on the bottom line. Compensation designs and develops systems, but has less control over the resulting use of the system than its sister functions of staffing and training. Wage and salary actions take place ceaselessly. The sheer volume of pay actions make it nearly impossible to prove causal connections. Nevertheless, the department should be able to show it has strongly influenced the utilization practices and the cost outcomes of the system, as well as the employees' satisfaction with their pay. If the results of those actions are positive, the compensation department can put together a strong case for its having contributed to lowering turnover and increasing morale and organizational effectiveness.

Benefits

The importance of benefits is clearly increasing. In 1940 the cost of the typical benefit program was approximately 5 percent of payroll. It wasn't until after World War II that "fringe" benefits became common. Between 1969 and 1980 a U.S. chamber of commerce survey showed that the average cost per employee for benefits had risen 297 percent. During the same period average weekly earnings had risen 223 percent. Informal surveys of participants in my workshops indicate that benefits commonly amount to 30 to 40 percent of salary. An expectation has developed that the organization must do more than pay an employee a salary. It must provide a financial security blanket in the form of health and life insurance; it must guarantee a comfortable retirement; it must pay tuition if an employee becomes a part-time student; and increasingly the organization is expected to provide extensive recreational and fitness facilities and programs. In short, the employer is being called on to play a multifaceted role in the life of the employee, somewhat akin to the government. With local and national governments cracking under the strain of years of deficit spending it appears that employers' involvement in the lives of their employees can only increase.

The purpose of the benefit program is to augment the salary program in its attempt to attract, retain, and incent employees. The question for us is how do we tell if the benefits department is operating efficiently and effectively? By their nature, benefits probably help to attract and retain, but I do not think they stimulate. Benefits play a background role. They are there when an employee needs them, and when they are not in use they tend to be forgotten. In one sense they are like lifeboats on an ocean liner. You may notice them when you come aboard, but they are ignored until they are needed. The job of benefits is to make sure that when employees need to use a benefit they find it readily accessible and able to provide a satisfactory solution to their problem. How well the benefits department accomplishes this objective is the subject of this chapter.

Cost is the most commonly discussed aspect of benefits. Premium costs, administrative costs, and staff costs are all considered part of the overall cost of benefits. However, there are other issues of importance if we want to consider return on investment. We noted above that benefits probably impact the organization's effort to attract and retain. The question is, how do we know which benefits do that most effectively? One way to answer that is to survey the employees. Another method, which is less obtrusive, is to study employees' participation and usage patterns. It seems logical that a program which addresses the needs of many employees much of the time will receive heavy usage. Another issue in our examination of the benefit staff's efficiency lies in the management of mandatory benefits and required filings. Plan maintenance is an unavoidable responsibility, and the timeliness of this activity can be tracked. Since benefits quickly fade into the recesses of the average employee's mind, communication programs are important. We will look at what and how benefits communications might take place. Finally, cost containment is one of the more unequivocal measures of department effectiveness. Given the ever-increasing cost of benefits, interest in cost control programs has added another dimension to the benefit manager's job.

FINDING THE TRUE COST OF BENEFITS

Everyone who works on benefits programs can tell you what percent of payroll these programs represent. It is important to keep that number visible because of the rate at which it is growing. No one can say what the number ought to be. It is a direct reflection of the employer's perception of his relationship with the employees, as well as the ability of the employer to purchase the benefit for the employees. There are two primary benefit cost measures from which all others emerge. They are the total cost and the support cost.

Total Cost

Most of the time when I ask someone what benefits cost their company they give me a number which represents the direct expenses associated with their various plans and programs. These are insurance premiums; vacation, holiday, and sick leave pay; tuition reimbursement; profit sharing; thrift and pension plans; and recreation programs. Those people who are meticulous will include legally mandated programs, such as FICA, unemployment insurance, workmen's compensation, and short-term disability. In addition, they will list discounts on employer goods or services, separation pay and moving expenses, paid breaks, jury duty, voting and bereavement time, service and suggestion awards, and other programs peculiar to their organization.

When both sets of numbers are combined the sum can be quite impressive. Yet, we still have only part of the expenses associated with benefits. The missing piece is the staff costs, overhead costs, and computer costs necessary to maintain the programs. These numbers, when added to benefit expenses, are also significant. There is no way to deny that they belong in any sum which purports to be the total cost of benefits. When insurance claims are handled by an outside organization the cost of that processing is almost always included. But, bring the work in-house, hire a staff, and give them space and equipment to do it, and it is forgotten. If the benefits program were shut down, people, space, and equipment costs would be eliminated immediately. By the same logic, so long as the program exists the support costs must be included.

Based on the foregoing, the computation for total benefit costs is illustrated in Formula C–7.

Total Benefits Cost

$$TBC = ST + OH + PC + PP + Misc \qquad (C\text{–}7)$$

where TBC = total costs of benefits

ST = staff time, staff hours spent on benefit planning and administration multiplied by salary and benefit hourly rates (e.g., $148,000)

OH = overhead expenses for space, furniture, equipment, etc. (e.g., $22,000)

PC = processing costs associated with benefit program administration (e.g., $84,000)

PP = plan payments, insurance and retirement and payments for government-mandated programs—including charges by external plan administrators, trustees, etc. (e.g., $19,810,000)

$Misc$ = vacation, holiday, sick leave, education, recreation, etc. (e.g., $9,047,000)

EXAMPLE

TBC = \$148,000 + \$22,000 + \$84,000 + \$19,810,000 + \$9,047,000
    = \$29,121,000

Two quick calculations from this number produce the two most commonly discussed numbers: cost per employee and percent of payroll.

Cost per Employee

$$BC/E = \frac{TBC}{e} \qquad (C-8)$$

where   BC/E = benefit cost per employee
         TBC = total cost of benefits (e.g., \$29,121,000)
           e = average number of employees (e.g., 3922)

EXAMPLE

$$BC/E = \frac{\$29,121,000}{3922}$$
$$= \$7425$$

Benefit to Payroll Ratio

$$B/P = \frac{TBC}{TSC} \qquad (C-9)$$

where   B/P = benefit to payroll ratio
        TBC = total cost of benefits
        TSC = total payroll cost (e.g., \$78,142,000)

EXAMPLE

$$B/P = \frac{\$29,121,000}{\$78,142,000}$$
$$= 37.2\%$$

PARTICIPATION PATTERNS

Most benefit packages include some choices for the employee. In fact, there is a definite trend toward more flexibility in plans. Employees today are generally better educated and better informed than they were in the 1930s, when benefit plans were still in their infancy. They are better equipped to make their own decisions about which benefits they want and need. So "cafeteria plans" are being tried by more companies each year. Most are designed to provide a security core of health and life insurance, while leaving many other options to the employees' choice. With the passage of legislation and pressure of unions and other outside social responsibility groups, many new optional plans are now available. Health maintenance organizations (HMOs) are one example. Thrift and profit-sharing plans, employee stock purchase plans, and educational reimbursements are others.

The benefits section can study which programs are desired by employees by watching what the usage rates are for basic plans (health and life insurances), as well as who participates in which optional programs. Periodically, the percent of participation or usage can be computed for a given benefit across different groups of employees. For example, you could look at the selection and usage of a particular benefit, such as an employee stock purchase plan, by exempt versus nonexempt employees. Or you could calculate usage by department or division. Age, sex, race, occupational groups, and other cuts are also possible. This type of analysis yields patterns which could help you design or redesign your benefit package into the most cost-effective system. Knowing usage patterns also helps you decide where to put your money when you decide it is time to upgrade your package.

One note about overreliance on participation patterns needs to be made. If a company does an ineffective job of communicating a benefit, employees may not be using it because they do not comprehend its purpose or value. It is possible that a feedback session with a representative group of employees will show that they misunderstood the program. Then a new communication can be planned with a subsequent pattern audit and feedback session.

Some companies add benefits which are currently fads without taking the time to find out what the current needs of their employees are. An additional benefit that comes from studying participation patterns is the creation of an early warning system. Some legislation-based programs require a broad usage of a plan by people at all levels across the organization. If you do not watch that, your organization may be rudely reminded of it by an auditing agency. This not only causes embarrassment for you and the company, but in case of some contributory programs, such as 401(C) income deferral plans, people may find their tax deferrals did not turn out to be what you told them to expect in the beginning. Effective benefits managers require use and participation studies before they recommend changes or additions to the current package and to make sure that everything is running the way it should.

MAINTENANCE

As benefits have become more complex, support activity has become not only more time consuming but also more important. Local and federal governments require a plethora of periodic reports. Both welfare and retirement plans must have reports prepared and mailed out to regulatory bodies. In the case of ERISA plans, there are also account status updates which must be sent out to plan participants.

All of these types of reporting have explicit deadlines associated with them. Governmental agencies require that your reports be mailed to them on time, whether or not anyone will review them at the agency on a timely basis. I have found the best way to ensure that the myriad of reports are filed on time is to develop a master calendar. Each filing would be listed on the calendar by title and receiving agency on the date it is due to be mailed. By referring to this tickler each week, my benefits manager could see what was due for preparation and mailing. If you are tightly staffed, everyone has a constant batch of brush fires to deal with and it is very easy to miss a filing date. With a reminder system the chances of that happening are greatly reduced.

Maintenance is an important activity for benefit systems. The manner and timeliness with which it is handled is an indication of your staff's efficiency.

EMPLOYEE COMMUNICATIONS

Another important activity is the employee benefits communication program, the aim of which is to improve your ROI for benefits. I use the term ROI because of the passive nature of benefits. I noted at the beginning of this chapter that benefits very quickly become background. People are always aware of how much their salary is and they know exactly when they are due for their next increase, but they usually forget about their benefit package until they need to use part of it. As a result, the organization does not receive a very healthy return from its considerable investment in benefits. In order to improve that situation the benefits manager needs to develop an active communications program.

There are many opportunities to communicate with employees. Here are some methods that are commonly used.

1. Orientation of new hires is your first opportunity to explain the package in detail.

2. Handbooks can be given out at orientation and updated as needed.

3. Brochures can be used in a variety of ways to describe individual plans or to present an overview.

4. Summary plan descriptions which are mandated provide the nuts and bolts of the various plans.

5. Posters and bulletin board announcements are very visible means of keeping employees aware of their many benefits.

6. Articles or a benefit column can be written for the employee newspaper.

7. Paycheck stuffers can be included in pay envelopes to remind employees about something that is timely.

8. Letters about issues such as coinsurance provisions can be mailed home where the spouse will see them.

9. Benefit bulletins and newsletters can be composed and distributed periodically.

10. Refresher/information meetings, during which employees can ask questions or receive updates, can be held at convenient times and places.

11. All-employee meetings can be scheduled to announce major changes and improvements.

12. Social security inquiry cards can be distributed to those who want to check the status of their account.

13. Open enrollment periods provide natural opportunities to review plan provisions or highlights.

14. Benefit fairs can be set up in cafeterias or meeting rooms where it is convenient for employees to inquire about a benefit or to browse to refresh their memory of what is available.

15. The annual benefit statement is considered by most people to be the most powerful communicative tool.

16. Video tapes can be produced and run during lunch periods in the corner of the cafeteria or in a conference room for employees who care to watch on their own.

This list is not all-inclusive. There are other things that can be done. The question is, how many are you doing now? If you are not doing at least 10, you probably are not operating an effective communications program.

COST CONTROL

From the end of World War II until about 1980 there was an uninter-rupted growth in benefit programs. I can remember operating under the mandate from management that we would improve our benefit package in some way at least once each year. With the slowdown of the early 1980s and the realization of how expensive the benefit package had become, many organizations reversed the 30-year trend and began to look seriously for ways to cut back plans or save money through administrative changes. It turned out that there are four opportunities for organizations to reduce benefit costs. They are found in:

- Plan design
- Plan administration
- Plan communication
- Plan financing

Before you launch into any major changes in the design, administra-tion, or communication of your benefit program it would be wise to consider what you are trying to achieve with benefits. Some companies have benefits simply because their competitors have them. Others know precisely why they have a certain mix of programs. It might save a lot of grief later if you can get management to sit down with you to discuss their rationale for benefits. Once you all know why you have certain things and what you hope to achieve by spending more or less money on one program versus another, you and your staff will know where to look for reductions, eliminations, modifications, or even en-hancements. It always pays to know where you are headed before you take off. As a wise armchair philosopher once asked, "if you don't know where you're going, how're you going to know if you're there when you get there?"

Plan Design

Practically speaking, it is very difficult to eliminate a longstanding benefit completely. Union contracts notwithstanding, employees come to expect a benefit as their right after it has been offered for a while. While it is not impossible to drop a benefit, you usually have to come up with something to offset it or face a morale problem that could cost you more in lost productivity than the expense of the benefit. Neverthe-less, there are some ways that you can directly reduce the cost of a benefit. First, you can introduce employee cost-sharing. On medical plans you can increase the employee's share of dependent coverage. You might be able to show employees that in order to maintain the same level of coverage as in the past they will have to contribute a couple of dollars for their own coverage this year. Legislation has come along in Sections 125 and 401(k) of the IRS code which permits employees to convert their sharing to pretax dollars. This makes it somewhat more attractive or at least acceptable to them.

Cafeteria approaches have added flexibility to benefit plan design. You can offer choices of two or more types of medical plans. Each plan would optimally serve the needs of different populations by offering the best ratio of care to cost based on individual need. If your plans are experience-rated, the result should be a lower overall cost.

Stay-well plans have been introduced in some organizations whereby employees who do not use their medical benefit can get a refund of some of the cost. These plans come in several variations and are being attempted in corporations, with differing degrees of success. The main concern with them is that people might not go to the doctor when they should. The result could be a severe problem later that might have been avoided if they had gone in the early stages of distress.

Another way to reduce cost and discourage unnecessary use of benefits is to tie the whole health-vacation-sick leave program together and cost it out to a total that is acceptable. If people use less than that total they can get some form of reward. However, this is a sensitive area, and a good deal of thought would need to go into the design of such a program.

The bottom line is that there is a strong trend toward individualism in designing plans these days. No longer do you have to have a benefits package that is a mirror image of some other organization's package. This calls for a new level of creativity, but it also offers another opportunity to demonstrate effective management of the benefits program.

Plan Administration

Chapter 10 will discuss administrative issues which deal with both efficiency and effectiveness. Beyond bookkeeping tasks there are other ways that you can assess your administration from the standpoint of cost containment.

When processing a coordination of benefits (COB) claim filed by the working spouse of one of your employees, you can use a "carve out" rule, in which your plan will pay only the difference between the benefit it would have provided and the benefit already provided by the other employer's plan. For example, if the spouse's plan would have covered $1200 of a $1500 claim and your plan would have done the same, normally you would pick up the $300 difference. With a carve out rule, you only pick up the uncovered amount up to your $1200 limit.

You can reduce or eliminate the ongoing expense of carrying retired or terminated employees who have very small balances in pension, profit-sharing, or thrift plans. For qualified plans, the law allows for speedy distribution of small balances through lump-sum payouts. A benefit consultant can help you set this procedure up. You can further reduce administrative expenses by reducing the number of choices in profit-sharing and thrift plans. Finally, you can limit the number of withdrawals or transfers during this year. All of these procedures take time and have little actual payoff for the company.

Probably one of the most effective activities you can get involved with is an employer group which acts to lobby and negotiate down the cost of health care. I believe that hospitals and clinics like to control costs also. If you can find ways of working with them to provide health care at lower costs to everyone, they are usually very receptive. They know they cannot go on escalating the cost of medical services. Some day, if they do not find ways to contain expenses, there will be a successful move by Congress to set up a national health plan. Most health-care facilities would not like to get involved with the bureaucracy which that implies.

Plan Communication

In the preceding section, I pointed out the many vehicles you can use to communicate benefits to your employees. By continually talking to and with employees about their benefits you involve them in the program. It becomes something which they participate in and not something which is handed to them without consideration for their perceived needs or interests. Besides informing them, the communication program should educate them. You can teach them something about how to deal with health care providers. Most people are intimidated by hospitals and doctors. You can teach them how to ask questions and give them the confidence of knowing that they have a right to the answers. You can also train supervisors on some of the rudiments of benefits. By having supervisors answer questions on the line, you save staff time and employee time, and you increase organizational productivity.

There is a trend toward health education in many organizations. Physical fitness programs, first aid, CPR, nutrition, and stress reduction are being taught. I cannot resist pointing out the paradox which exists in companies who spend time and money on stress-management programs and then send employees back into units where the organizational philosophy and operating practices create unnecessary and unreasonable amounts of physical and emotional stress. It is somewhat akin to giving a person a snake-bite kit before throwing them into a pit full of rattlesnakes.

Plan Financing

Alternative plan financing offers many opportunities to quickly and directly reduce benefits costs. It was not too long ago that almost all organizations carried standard full-cost insurance programs for health, disability, workers compensation, and life coverage for their employees. They paid their premiums faithfully and hoped that experience would keep the rates from rising too much. In the late 1970s, more companies started to experiment with alternative financing arrangements. Minimum premium contracts, administrative-services-only contracts (ASO) and self-insured plans became more widespread. In almost all cases these procedures for funding insurance programs have proved to be money savers. They eliminate prefunding of reserves for claims. Self-insured plans and ASOs eliminate state premium taxes as well as the risk and reserve charges of the carrier. In the early years, only the larger companies tried these options. Lately, I have talked with people in organizations with less than 200 employees who are taking advantage of them. The risks of self-insuring can be covered by an inexpensive stop-loss policy which covers you in case of extraordinary claims. Because of this growing trend, insurance carriers are not nearly as arbitrary as they were up to about 1975. They are vulnerable and they know it. If you do your homework and negotiate strongly, you can usually find ways to get the benefits you want at something less than the "sticker price."

In many companies, the cost of pension plans has become a burden. There are at least three ways you can reduce that burden for your organization. Here again is a case where good benefits consultants earn their fees by helping you choose among funding methods. Depending on the growth profile of your company, funding alternatives can save you a lot of money now and in the future. Another area the consultant can help you with is the choice of how to amortize past service liabilities. The shortest amortization period permitted is 10 years, and the longest is 30 years. The difference in the amortization payment between the two extremes can be as much as 40 percent. The third way consultants can help, if they have a financial background, is to guide you in deciding on the timing of funding. Depending on your organization's cash flow, profit picture, and ability or need for tax deductions, you can time your funding to take best advantage of the situation. If you are having a particularly profitable year, you might want to prefund certain liabilities. This contribution offsets some of your income and reduces your tax rate. In slower years you might want to stretch out the contribution as long as possible to preserve cash for operations.

There are many ways to manipulate the financing of your various plans. Choosing the alternatives which best suit your current and future needs can significantly impact the organization's bottom line profits. If after a year of self-insuring a disability or health plan you can go to the CEO and show that you have saved the company thousands of dollars, there will be no question about whether or not you are doing an effective job of managing benefits.

SUMMARY

Organizations spend a great deal of money on benefits. There is a strong push in the United States to continually expand the private sector's involvement in benefits. It will probably happen even more as the federal government finds itself less able to provide services without additional deficit spending. It behooves benefits managers to deal with this trend by reviewing the way their function operates. It is incumbent on them to be cost-effective managers and to be able to show the top executives how the organization can improve its ROI in benefits.

Claim and Record Processing

Processing lends itself to measurement. Paper processing is a very visible activity wherein items flow along a predictable path toward a predetermined goal. They usually pause at certain points in the journey for someone to treat them. The treatments may mean adding data, extracting information for another use, or modifying or deleting data. A document may reach a decision point where someone decides that, in whole or in part, it should either continue in its current direction, go off into another process chain, or dump its data and be discarded. Eventually documents conclude their journey in a file cabinet, a wastebasket, or in the hands of the customer. All of these actions can be measured in terms of quantity, time, cost, or quality. These facts apply whether one considers accounting, purchasing, personnel records, benefits claims, or any other business paper processing. Both efficiency and effectiveness indices can be developed. Measures of efficiency deal with volume, errors, throughput time, and cost. Measures of effectiveness describe levels of satisfaction or customer complaints.

COUNTING VOLUME

A natural place to start measuring a process is volume count. This quantity indicator tells you how much is being handled. It can be expressed in several ways. You can count number of documents handled or number of entries made. If you were looking at insurance claims, you might count number of claims processed. You could differentiate claims by type since some are more complicated than others. For example, coinsurance claims take more time than standard one-carrier claims. If you were looking at employee records, you might want to count number of entries.

A records clerk will sometimes make several additions or changes to a record at one sitting. Frequently, an employee may transfer between departments and be promoted at the same time. This requires a new department number, job title, salary, and performance review date. Since this case is clearly more complex than a simple address change, it makes sense to count number of entries or changes rather than number of files processed. By tracking how many transactions an efficient records clerk or claims administrator can handle daily, weekly, or monthly, it is possible to set the optimum staffing level for a given volume of work.

You can also project the number of processors required if you look at past history. If experience shows that you generally have 0.25 record changes per employee per month, you can predict your future workload by examining the projected employee level in future months. For example, using the 0.25 factor, the addition of 100 employees in the organization means 25 extra changes to handle. Formula C–10 shows the computation for volume processing.

Volume Processing

$$CPR = \frac{R}{S} \qquad (C-10)$$

where   CPR = claims processing rate
   R = total records processed (e.g., 850)
   S = average number of staff processors (e.g., 3)

EXAMPLE

$$CPR = \frac{850}{3}$$
$$= 283.3$$

There is a handy format for keeping track of claim processing volume. Figure 10.1 shows the amount of activity by type each month and a running year-to-date (YTD) total. Through observation of past efficiency levels you have determined that a processor can handle a certain number of transactions per month (283). When your workload reaches or exceeds that level you know automatically that it is time to consider an addition to staff in records.

Consistent use of such yardsticks takes the guesswork out of staffing.

Month		New hires	Term	Prom	Trans	Salary increase	Employee changes	Totals
Jan		98	80	52	87	208	88	613
	YTD*	98	80	52	87	208	88	613
Feb		63	51	69	29	214	36	462
	YTD	161	131	121	110	422	124	1075
Mar		54	75	84	55	254	40	562
	YTD	215	206	205	165	676	164	1637
Apr		119	70	164	78	281	55	767
	YTD	334	276	369	243	957	219	2404
May		96	62	104	70	217	89	638
	YTD	430	338	473	313	1174	308	3042
Jun		136	70	93	73	411	66	849
	YTD	566	408	566	386	1585	374	3891
Jul		174	75	82	61	398	64	854
	YTD	740	483	648	447	1983	438	4745
Aug		182	77	171	67	377	65	939
	YTD	922	560	819	514	2360	503	5684
Sep		144	88	88	181	194	118	813
	YTD	1066	648	907	695	2554	621	6497
Oct		152	90	90	80	310	78	811
	YTD	1218	738	997	775	2864	699	7298
Nov		160	92	91	78	389	81	891
	YTD	1378	830	1088	853	3253	780	8189
Dec		165	95	103	84	302	88	837
1982 TOTALS		1543	925	1191	937	3555	868	9026

* Year to date.

Figure 10.1 Record Processing Table

Most organizations are reluctant to add employees in staff departments, but this approach helps you justify without argument the need for more human resources.

In the insurance claim area, another way of looking at efficiency is the amount of time that elapses from the day that a claim is filed until a check is received by the employee. This is in part also a way to increase or maintain positive employee attitudes toward the insurance program. Long delays in payment generate morale problems.

In this case the measurement, shown in Formula C–11, is a simple subtraction problem.

$$T = DP - DR \qquad (C\text{–}11)$$

where   T = turnaround time
   DP = date claim paid (e.g., September 20)
   DR = date claim received (filed) (e.g., September 10)

EXAMPLE

$$T = 20 - 10$$
$$= 10 \text{ days}$$

Whenever contracts are being let with insurance carriers or claims administrators an agreement should be reached on turnaround time. It should either be written into the contract or put into an agreement letter. Any reputable administrator should be willing to stipulate that, 95 percent of the time, standard, one-carrier claims will be paid within X days. If you do partial processing of claims in your benefit office before forwarding them to the administrator, you should set your internal processing standard as well.

ERRORS

A final efficiency measure which has a qualitative aspect to it is error rate. The ratio of errors to total claims processed should be extremely low. The consequence of an error is more than rework: it usually causes a morale problem. Employees whose claims are short-changed or even overpaid quickly lose respect for the competence of the benefits staff. Formula C–12 gives the calculation for error rate.

$$ER = \frac{RC}{CP} \qquad (C\text{–}12)$$

where   ER = error rate
   RC = rejected claims (e.g., 5)
   CP = total claims processed (e.g., 650)

EXAMPLE

$$ER = \frac{5}{650}$$
$$= 0.007\%$$

COMPUTING COSTS

Cost can be viewed from one perspective, the initial question being unit cost. That is, what does it cost to process one claim or make one change to a document, such as an employee record? Since transactions vary in complexity you will have to develop an average unit cost. The first step is to observe the operation and record how long, on the average, it takes to complete whatever the task is. This can be done by a supervisor, an industrial engineer, or the operator performing the task. There are obvious pros and cons for each approach. As manager, the decision is yours. If an operator is doing nothing but processing, you can count the hours spent at the job and divide by the number of transactions completed. This results in an average transaction time. However, if the operator also answers phones or is interrupted by other people or other tasks, then an individual transaction time log must be kept. Whichever system you use, in order to obtain a truly representative time you will have to collect data at different times of the day, week, and month. Fluctuations due to workload, fatigue, interruptions, or other variables have to be normalized. After you have dealt with all these issues you will be rewarded with a solid, dependable, average transaction time measure. All that remains is to apply cost variables to it.

Costs are essentially those expenses associated with staff time and overhead. For example, the hourly numbers might be

Average operator's salary	$5.00
Average operator's benefits	1.80
Overhead	1.10
Cost of supervision per operator	1.40
(Supervisor salary divided by number supervised)	
Average cost of processing	$9.30

Given this you can compute the cost of processing, as shown in Formula C–13.

$$PC/T = \frac{ST + OH + MT}{P/h} \qquad \text{(C–13)}$$

where   PC/T = processing cost per transaction
ST = staff time, salary and benefits (e.g., $6.80)
OH = overhead (e.g., $1.10)
MT = management time, cost of supervision (e.g., $1.40)
P/h = number of items processed per hour (e.g., 20)

EXAMPLE

$$PC/T = \frac{\$6.80 + \$1.10 + \$1.40}{20}$$
$$= \frac{\$9.30}{20}$$
$$= \$0.465$$

Knowing the cost of processing is important from a managerial standpoint. A basic question for benefit managers is, "should we process insurance claims ourselves, or should we contract that out to an insurance company or claims administration company?" In order to make that decision it is necessary to know what it costs to process employee insurance claims internally. In this example the processing clerk is making 20 changes to the records per hour. If we were looking at insurance claims instead, we might find a much slower pace throughout since claims are more complicated than records. Therefore, a rate of four per hour might be satisfactory. The setting of performance standards is a local issue. The rate will depend on the forms used, the amount of automation involved, the total range of tasks to be performed, and extraneous matters such as interruptions.

There are other issues, such as turnaround time, employee relations, and control, that are part of the decision. It may even be decided that cost is less important than employee relations or timeliness. Nevertheless, an appropriate choice is hard to make without all the facts, and cost is an essential variable in the mix.

RECORDS COST

The cost of maintaining organizational records is seldom discussed. It is assumed to be a necessary and unavoidable part of doing business, and in fact it is. Yet, like any other aspect of business it deserves an occasional review.

I believe that we ought to know what it costs our organization to maintain records. My experience is that the number is sufficiently large to deserve attention. Secondly, it is often large enough to become a target for a cost reduction project. Since record systems are in most cases either wholly or partially paper-dependent, the question of automation is becoming increasingly prevalent. Microfiche and computer systems are moving inexorably into what was previously a paper domain. As technology continues to present cost-effective solutions we will undoubtedly see electricity and silicon supplant ink and paper as record system media.

In most cases we have looked at activities from the standard input/ output ratio. Here we are interested only in the input. What is it costing us to maintain records? The answer is simple. Our cost inputs are staff, equipment (computers, microfiche, etc.), supplies, and facilities. Facility costs for space, heat, light, etc., may be considered a given and not included—that is a matter of choice. The percent of total department costs that record keeping costs represent is shown in Formula C–14.

Record Keeping Costs

$$RC = \frac{ST + EC + S + OH}{DC} \qquad (C–14)$$

where $RC =$ record keeping costs
$ST =$ staff time, salary, benefits, and misc. (e.g., $85,200)
$EC =$ equivalent costs, purchase, depreciation, and operating costs for machines, desks, file cabinets, etc. [e.g., $42,500]
$S =$ supplies (e.g., $13,800)
$OH =$ overhead (e.g., $14,650)
$DC =$ total department expenses (e.g., $1,200,000)

EXAMPLE

$$RC = \frac{\$85,200 + \$42,500 + \$13,800 + \$14,650}{\$1,200,000}$$

$$= \frac{\$156,150}{\$1,200,000}$$

$$= 13.0\%$$

Once you have all the numbers together, opportunities for cost reduction and better utilization of resources may become apparent. Even if the first result is satisfactory and offers little room for improvement, by tracking this percentage annually you will be able to maintain it within an acceptable range.

SATISFACTION FACTOR

The final, and in some ways one of the more important, measures in the processing business is employee satisfaction. Prompt attention, rapid turnaround, and accurate processing are all expected, whether it be an insurance claim or a change to an employee record. Usually there is no question about employee or managerial satisfaction. If your benefits staff is not operating at peak efficiency, you will probably hear about it. Satisfaction can be calculated as a ratio of complaints to volume, as shown in Formula C–15.

Claims Satisfaction

$$CS = \frac{C}{P} \qquad \text{(C–15)}$$

where   CS = degree of employee satisfaction with settlement of their claims

C = total claims contested (e.g., 8)

P = total claims processed (e.g., 650)

EXAMPLE

$$CS = \frac{8}{650}$$
$$= 1.2\%$$

There is no norm to which you can compare your experience. One contested claim is too much, yet it seems inevitable that a very small percentage will be contested. Prompt, fair, and full treatment of the contested claim is the best that you can do.

AUDITING ADMINISTRATION

No administrative system or staff is perfect. An administrative audit usually turns up procedural errors or omissions which can be corrected to save time and money. We have talked about errors and satisfaction. Tightening up on lax procedures reduces errors and increases employee satisfaction. You might find small savings coming from arithmetic errors. You might also find that a clerk is not well trained and is paying for services not covered in the plan or paying more than is allowed. It is possible that ineligible people are being covered. An employee who does not have dependent coverage may be having children or spouse claims paid because no one checked the record. If you have a claim processing system where employees file directly with the carrier or service company, you could learn that terminated people are still filing and getting paid. Organizations which are very large or spread out across several states often find that changes in coverage and eligibility have not kept up or have never been made. Normally, administrative errors such as these do not cost a significant amount of money. Nevertheless, administrative procedures and records should be audited periodically just to keep the system operating smoothly. You want the organization to have confidence in your administrative system. Judiciously applied audits will help develop and maintain that confidence.

SUMMARY

Whether you think of processing from the viewpoint of claims or records, the measures are basically similar. The only significant differences will be the results. Since claims are more complex, they take longer to process and are usually susceptible to higher error rates. The main point is that standards of performance can be set by which your staff's output can be evaluated.

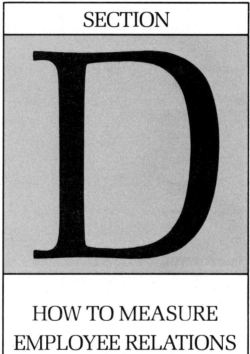

SECTION

D

HOW TO MEASURE
EMPLOYEE RELATIONS
ACTIVITIES

Orientation and Counseling

Employee relations suffers from an identity crisis. The annual American Society for Personnel Administration-Bureau of National Affairs (ASPA-BNA) survey of personnel activities, budgets, and staffs lists 46 activities for which the personnel department has all or some responsibility. Nearly 30 percent of those are usually handled by employee relations. As if that were not enough, the range of activities covers such dissimilar tasks as new hire orientation, unemployment compensation administration, recreation and social programs, counseling, employee communications, suggestion systems, and food service. It is this heterogeneous mix which gets in the way of clearly describing what the function is all about. The diversity of jobs demands a range of skills unequalled by any other human resources function. It seems that when someone comes up with another task that has to get done, if it is not clearly an employment, compensation, or training matter, employee relations gets it. The department can justifiably be described as a catch-all. Given its scope, it is difficult to know where to start and what to include. It is impractical to attempt the measurement of better than a dozen different tasks. Clearly, we must be selective. We must pick those activities which we believe are the more important ones and focus our efforts on them. I have chosen to look at five issues: new hire orientation, counseling, absence, turnover, and unemployment compensation administration. I will briefly discuss grievances in the counseling section also.

GETTING STARTED

New hire orientation is an activity which is seldom subjected to measurement. One of the reasons is that the objectives of orientation are often not clear. Generally speaking, we assume that we orient new employees to speed their integration into the organization. That is a rather difficult result to isolate and evaluate. For many years HR department staffs complained that they could not get supervisors to send new hires to the orientation session. This is no longer the case in most organizations. Today, most companies require a new hire to attend some type of formal orientation program shortly after they report for work. The length, format, and date of the program varies widely among organizations, but the old problem of attendance is largely a thing of the past.

In most companies new hire orientation has become an act of faith. As such, it is almost impossible to assess its effectiveness. If measurement is desired, then some sort of cost and impact goals must be specified beforehand. Given a set of desired outcomes, a program can be designed to evaluate whether or not they were achieved.

Tim Gallwey, in his book *Inner Game of Tennis,*[1] writes that people learning a new skill often push themselves to a point of dysfunctionality. They try so hard that they overplay. What Gallwey is pointing out is the inverse relationship which occurs at a certain point between motivation and effectiveness. Economists call it the point of diminishing returns.

This same syndrome is observable with new employees. They arrive the first day in a positive frame of mind, highly motivated to work, and somewhat confused by the new setting. During the first few hours on the job many employees are intimidated by the strange environment, and a new hire orientation program is an excellent way to deal with this problem. By putting employees at ease and helping them to be mentally alert yet relaxed, they learn faster, make fewer mistakes, and generally develop on-the-job confidence.

One major electronics company has a secondary orientation which takes place on the job. It goes beyond the general program which is designed to communicate information needed by all employees. This departmental orientation covers issues indigenous to the department. Five subjects are discussed:

1. Jargon.   New hires are taught the company's and the department's language. Every industry and every organization has a language of its own. New employees are often confused, embarrassed, and make mistakes simply because they do not understand the language.

2. People. The orientation discusses the kinds of people with whom the new employee must deal. Idiosyncracies, styles, and personalities are covered so that the person knows what to expect and can figure out how to work effectively with new coworkers.

3. Resources. The new employee is shown where to find the tools and supplies needed to do the job. Information is also provided on the administrative procedures which need to be followed in order to obtain these items.

4. Problems. Every organization has problems. This company tells people what kinds of problems they can expect to encounter. It also teaches them acceptable ways to handle the resulting frustrations.

5. Priorities. Last, and probably most important, the goals of the work group and the company are explained. The purpose is to let the employee know where to focus his or her energies in both the short and the long run.

The end product of this secondary orientation is a new employee who adjusts to a strange environment quickly.

ORIENTATION COST

Since orientation is a discrete, identifiable event, it's relatively easy to measure. Cost can be measured at three levels: cost per employee, cost per department, and cost of staff time to orient. The first measure is cost per employee, as shown in Formula ER–1.

Orientation Cost per Employee

$$OC/E = \frac{[T \times (R/h \times E)] + DC}{E} \qquad (ER\text{–}1)$$

where OC/E = average cost to orient an employee
        T = time spent in orientation (e.g., 4 hours)
   R/h = average hourly pay rate of attending employees (e.g., \$8.25)*
     DC = HR department cost per employee (e.g., \$195)
      E = total number of employees oriented (e.g., 20)

*Pay rates should include benefits also.

EXAMPLE

$$OC/E = \frac{[4 \times (\$8.25 \times 20)] + \$195}{20}$$

$$= \frac{\$855}{20}$$

$$= \$42.75$$

This basic ratio can be computed by using either actual hourly rates of each new hire or, more easily, by using an average hourly rate for each job group represented in the orientation. If this task were done on the job by the local supervisor it would cost more to obtain the same level of indoctrination. Supervisors and managers usually do not know corporate policies as well as the employee relations staff and therefore cannot give the same quality of information in the same time frame. This cost is part of the cost of turnover. It goes into the indirect cost line on the turnover cost estimator to be discussed later in this section.

The second cost measure, cost per department, deals with the lost productivity which a department suffers when the new hire is in orientation. Since this is a total cost and not a ratio calculation, the calculation, as shown in Formula ER–2, is a straight multiplication problem.

Departmental Orientation Cost

$$OC/D = TO \times R/h \times N \qquad \text{(ER–2)}$$

where OC/D =   orientation cost per department
   TO =   time spent in orientation
   R/h =   average hourly rate (e.g., \$8.25)
   N =   number of new hires in orientation from a given department (e.g., 5)

EXAMPLE

$$OC/D = 4 \times \$8.25 \times 5$$
$$= \$165$$

This formula can be extended to the total organization. If the orientation were taking place within the department, the cost of lost supervisor time would have to be added in. So, while at first glance it may seem like a significant amount of wage and salary time is being lost by production to orientation, when the cost of many supervisors' time is added in it is clear that handling the process in the HR department is more efficient. The third cost measure, cost of staff time as shown in Formula ER–3, makes this point clear.

HR Department Orientation Expense

$$SOC/H = \frac{T \times R/h}{N} \qquad (ER\text{-}3)$$

where   SOC/H = staff orientation cost per new hire
         T = time spent preparing and conducting orientation (e.g., 5 hours)
       R/h = average hourly rate of HR department staff, including benefits (e.g., $12.20)
         N = number of new hires oriented (e.g., 20)

EXAMPLE

$$SOC = \frac{5 \times \$12.20}{20}$$
$$= \frac{\$61.00}{20}$$
$$= \$3.05$$

Clearly, a supervisor cannot orient a new hire for something like $3.05. The issue of quality of the orientation does not even have to be discussed when the cost disparity is as great as it obviously is here.

EVALUATING THE IMPACT

As in most cases, the result is at least as important an issue as is the cost of an activity. I have always wanted to know the employee reactions to our orientation program. I suspect that you do too. An easy way to learn that is through a simple survey. A sample of this kind of survey is shown in Fig. 11.1. These are some of the basic questions which a recent hire can respond to accurately and without any fear. By making the name optional you will probably get the most truthful results. So long as you have a job title and department number you can trace back any problems that may show up.

In my opinion the most valuable question is number 4. We both know that there are supervisors and managers in every company who believe that they are the sole authority on everything in their department. If they are administering policy and procedures in a manner contrary to company intent, you will want to know about it. You have probably experienced supervisors who take a new employee under their wing on the first day and say something like, "I know what they told you in orientation. But let me show you how things really work

To assist us in evaluating our New Employee Orientation Program, please complete the questions below and return to Personnel. You need not sign your name, but please indicate your job title, department, and the requested dates.

Instructions: Circle the number that best describes your feelings about each statement below. For instance, if you strongly agree with the statement, circle number 6; if you mildly disagree with the statement, circle number 3; etc.

	Strongly disagree	Disagree	Mildly disagree	Mildly agree	Agree	Strongly agree
1. I felt very welcome and at home after my orientation.	1	2	3	4	5	6
2. The information I needed to know on the following subjects was clearly provided:						
(a) Insurance and benefits	1	2	3	4	5	6
(b) Familiarity with the facility	1	2	3	4	5	6
(c) Policies and rules	1	2	3	4	5	6
(d) Affirmative action plan	1	2	3	4	5	6
(e) Safety/security	1	2	3	4	5	6
(f) Forms and records	1	2	3	4	5	6
3. The orientation leader was well informed and answered my questions.	1	2	3	4	5	6
4. What I was told at orientation proved to be accurate in my daily work.	1	2	3	4	5	6
5. I learned in orientation where to find the additional information I might need.	1	2	3	4	5	6

Comments or suggestions: _____

_____

_____

_____   _____
Name (optional)   Job title   Dept. #

_____   _____
Date of orientation   Date questionnaire returned

Figure 11.1 Orientation Survey

out here." If that is going on, you may find out about it through a survey.

COUNSELING: THE EARLY WARNING SYSTEM

Counseling of employees, supervisors, and managers has no beginning and no end. It is a continuous process which can and does take place anywhere at any time. The counseling staff cannot go a day without someone stopping them somewhere for information or advice. No place is sacred, no place secure from the person who needs counseling or who wants to lodge a complaint. The counselor has to deal with employees in the office, the hallway, the shop floor, the cafeteria, the parking lot, and even sometimes in the restroom.

A situation like this defies most attempts at measurement. It makes data collection an almost insurmountable problem. The nature of a great deal of counseling rules out the usual forms of effectiveness evaluation. The only practical way to deal with this dynamic, amorphous phenomenon is to start at the beginning.

Since counseling does take place everywhere at any time, data collection is difficult. If counselors counseled only in their offices it would be relatively easy to keep track of the number, type, and time of counseling sessions. Since much counseling is unplanned and away from the office, there is the belief that accurate records cannot be kept. That is true, in part. The standard method of record keeping on counseling is to create a simple log which has columns for name, department, type of counseling (the subject), time spent, action taken, and whatever else might be desired. Since this log is usually of some size it is inconvenient for the counselors to carry it everywhere they go. As counselors walk about the organization they may counsel with several people on different subjects for different periods of time before they return to their office. There is no easy way they can log all pertinent data as they go. When they return to their office they may get involved in other duties and forget to log the talks. Therefore, there will always be some margin of error. But, valuable record keeping of counseling sessions is not as far off as people might think.

Have you ever noticed how well a professional athlete remembers minute details of the sporting event just completed? A golfer can tell you exactly where every shot in the past round landed, what club was used, which way the wind was blowing, and so on. A baseball player can talk you through an entire game, recounting what each batter did. This memory skill is not confined to athletes. Anyone who is concentrating on their job can demonstrate amazing recall. After several years of observing and checking with employee counselors, we estimated that they were about 95 percent accurate in their recall of all sessions. They almost always remembered who they talked to, what departments the employees were from, and what the subject was. They were about 90 percent accurate in recalling the amount of time spent per session. These people were just as professional in their work as any athlete. Their dedication to their job and their interest in maintaining the system was such that they were able to keep very accurate information on counseling.

Before you are misled into believing it is no problem at all, let me confess that it took some time for the counselors to reach high levels of precision. In the beginning they openly opposed the idea, and the excuses they used were numerous. The turning point came when they began to believe in the value of keeping the data. Shortly after the counselors started turning in their monthly consolidated report they saw the benefit to themselves and to the department. They could see just how much they had accomplished the previous month. They began to see trends which we all used to head off problems before they became unmanageable. The longer this went on the more value they found in the reports. As they came to realize the benefit, they sharpened up their memories. Within just a few months they stopped talking about the extra work involved. They gave up the belief that the data would be inaccurate. Their skepticism about how the information would be used disappeared. From then on we never worried about the validity and reliability of the counseling report. The key here, as in all other attempts to persuade people to do something, is to lead them to see the benefit in doing it. Reasonable people will respond when they are shown the payoff.

As I mentioned earlier, the best way to run a measurement system is to have everyone collect as much of their own data as possible. At the end of a reporting period the data can be picked up by one person and put into a consolidated report. One of the most comprehensive report forms in the system is the employee relations counseling summary shown in Fig. 11.2. The counseling summary contains four categories of information. First, across the top it lists the types of counseling subjects covered. This list is based on experience. If you keep track of your counseling by subject matter for a month or two you will be able to consolidate it into a manageable number of categories. Down the left side you put in the departments, job groups, levels, or other classifications of employees who used the service. The most common way to do this is to list departments. If your system is computerized you could sort it by as many categories as you have identified in the computer. The greater the number of sorts, the greater the value of the information.

Subject / Department	Problem with Supervisor	Personal problems	Problem with job	Career counseling	Transfer counseling	Leave of absence	Problem with employees	Policies and procedures advice	Legal/ equal employment	Exit interviews	Number of contacts	Number of hours
Administration												
Accounting												
Data Processing												
Other												
Manufacturing												
Assembly												
Test												
Shipping												
Maintenance												
Marketing												
Advertising												
Product Development												
Sales												
Research and development												
Total												
Comments												

Figure 11.2   Employee Relations Counseling Summary

Ultimately, the purpose of this data collection is to provide you with an early warning system that keeps the company out of trouble. By seeing trends early you can react before there is a major problem. Looking inside the cells you see they are divided. The subdivisions are for the number of contacts made per subject and the number of hours spent discussing the subject. The far right column is a total contacts and hours summary by classification.

When this report is filled out for all counseling conducted during the month you may find that there are a few blank cells. That is all right because problems tend to run in cycles, and from time to time a particular issue is not a question or a problem for some departments. Overall, the filled-in form has an overwhelming amount of data. Careful reading will disclose a richness of information which will point the manager directly toward the most pressing issues of the day.

ANALYSIS CALCULATIONS

You can do an eyeball analysis of the data on the summary form and pick up most of the pertinent information. However, if you have this system automated you can run a few other computations which will add to your understanding of the environment. My experience has shown me that an in-depth analysis of counseling data is a much more accurate display of the state of mind of the employees than is an attitude survey. Without going into this issue at length, let me just make some points about attitude surveys. First, attitudes surveys suffer from a number of inherent weaknesses. Here are a few:

1. Unless you have norms against which to measure the results they are of little value. Numbers are relative, which means that you need comparative numbers from repeated surveying. But, if you survey every 2 years, your population may have changed as much as 25 percent. The remaining 75 percent may have changed their idea of what is acceptable and so they are also different people.

2. A corollary is that surveys are a snapshot of one day in the life of an employee. Many extraneous issues may influence the responses. Something as unrelated as a fight with a spouse that morning can turn an otherwise satisfied employee into a complainer.

3. Surveys supplied by outside companies may offer regional or national norms against which you can compare your responses. Who cares? No other company has the same mix of people, products, objectives, philosophy, style, etc., as yours. Outside norms are weak at best.

4. Unless your responses have an importance scale built in, it is hard to tell whether or not you need to respond to a low score. Maybe employees do not like something and maybe they do not really give a darn besides.

5. All survey methods suffer from weaknesses of validity and reliability because they survey human beings. People are mercurial. They change. Some are even too frightened or too paranoid to give honest responses.

6. Finally, after decades of research which have resulted in a great deal of ambiguity about attitudes, Fishbein and Ajzen[2] tell it like it is.

> Unfortunately, despite the vast amount of research and publication . . . on the topic, there is little agreement about what an attitude is, how it is formed or changed, and what role, if any, it plays in influencing or determining behavior.

The use of attitude surveys in industry, in most cases, is an example of how "pop psychology" has been introduced by people who do not have the knowledge or experience to practice the science. It seems to me that until the day comes when companies are committed enough to hire professionals and to support valid research projects we are better off dealing with what employees do than with what they think.

Formulas ER–4 through ER–6 provide examples of the several perspectives used in analyzing counseling. Formula ER–4 takes department population into consideration. In effect, it weights the volume of counseling by department size so that each department can be viewed relative to other departments.

Departmental Counseling Factor

$$DCF = \frac{SD}{DP} \qquad \text{(ER–4)}$$

where   DCF = departmental counseling factor
        SD = sessions per department (e.g., 80)
        DP = department population (e.g., 360)

EXAMPLE

$$DCF = \frac{80}{360}$$
$$= 22\%$$

This measure allows two types of analysis. First, how much counseling is taking place relative to other departments? Second, is the trend increasing or decreasing overall? It is a volume analysis and does not segregate sessions by type as does Formula ER–5.

Counseling Topic Factor

$$TP = \frac{T}{SD} \qquad \text{(ER–5)}$$

where   TP = percentage of each topic discussed
        T = number of sessions on that topic (e.g., 20)
        SD = total sessions for the department (e.g., 140)

EXAMPLE

$$TP = \frac{20}{140}$$
$$= 14.2\%$$

This measure will reveal the topic which is coming up the most. When tracked from month to month, it will show any trends in counseling topics. It can also be compared across departments to see if a topic is a concern for the whole organization or only isolated departments.

Another issue besides number of contacts is the amount of time being spent by topic and in total. Time is probably the more important issue since it usually indicates the severity of the concern. We found that the relationship of contacts to time also was interesting to watch. If you look at the average time per topic over several reporting periods, you may find it increasing or decreasing at a significant rate. These early warning signs are most valuable for the employee relations manager who is trying to be proactive.

Counseling Topic Time

$$\text{CTT} = \frac{\text{ST}}{\text{N}} \qquad \qquad \text{(ER–6)}$$

where CTT = average time per topic
        TT = total session time per topic (e.g., 15 hours)
        N = number of sessions per topic (e.g., 25 sessions)

EXAMPLE

$$\text{CTT} = \frac{15 \text{ hours}}{25 \text{ sessions}}$$

$$= 0.60 \text{ hours per session (36 minutes)}$$

This same formula can be used in aggregate to measure the average session time for all sessions. This gives you an overall feeling of the level of intensity. However, the most useful application is as shown above.

These measures can be used for classifications other than departments. So long as you have the capability to do multiple sortings of the data, you can apply these measures to levels (exempt and non-exempt), job groups (programmers, assemblers, accountants, etc.), or EEO-affected categories. The more sortings you can compute the more data you have to manage the problems.

At the beginning of this section you saw a summary table of counseling data which presented a great deal of information. Its only weakness is that it shows only one month's activity. There are other formats which also provide a full breakdown and have the bonus of showing more than one month at a time. Figure 11.3 is a bar graph which gives you a 3-month perspective. Each month you drop off the oldest month and add in the newest one. Bar graphs offer the advantage of being able to show trends very quickly. In Fig. 11.3 you can see that problems with employees and exit interviews have both risen dramatically over the

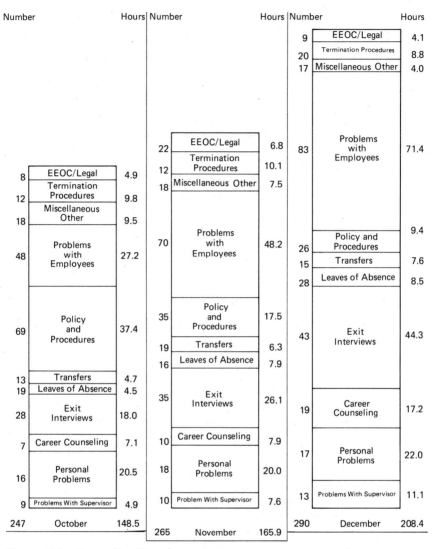

Figure 11.3 Counseling Trends

3 months displayed. Conversely, policy and procedures questions have fallen from 37.4 hours to 9.4 in 3 months.

Given the first issue of rising rates you could go to the employee relations staff and ask them what is happening. They can check their logs and usually pinpoint the sources. They may say that the problems are spread across the organization. Or they may say that they are pretty much confined to a given department or group of people. Once they isolate the source you can usually do something to fix the problem or to have someone else fix it.

When you do solve a problem, you see the results in examples such as the policy and procedures trend. For instance, if you hire a large number of new employees and supervisors over a short period of time, you may find them beseiging your staff with policy questions. Then it is a simple matter to run a training program for supervisors and watch the volume go down. By calculating the time, and thus the dollars, wasted in October versus December you can show a quick cost-benefit analysis of your training class. And remember, it takes two to talk. The 37.4 hours in October only covers the person with the problem. While they were off the job talking with your staff, your people were also precluded from doing something else productive. Hence, the production time lost was really 37.4 X 2, or 74.8. Time is money, and by multiplying 74.8 by the salary rates of your people and the complainants you have the cost of the problem. Then, when you multiply the December rate of 9.4 X 2 X the salaries involved, you have the difference that the training made. It is a simple method which will not stun your audience with its impact. But, it will show that you are making a contribution and that you are bottom-line oriented.

There is one note of caution with this bar graph or with any calculation of counseling time. While you may see counseling employees as serving a useful purpose, some managers view it as wasted time. They see it as an excuse for an employee to take some time off their job and shoot the breeze with your staff. You must be able to assure them that this is worthwhile time and that your staff does not conduct coffee klatches to keep the employees amused. You can point out that if your staff was not dealing with issues that the supervisors obviously cannot, the problems would remain unresolved. They might seem to disappear, but actually they go underground if they are not addressed properly. So, instead of one employee being off the job talking about a concern and getting professional help, there would be two or more employees off-line probably making a molehill into a mountain.

It is a great temptation once you have your system up and running to go skipping up to the boss's office and declare how well the system is operating. Just remember, the boss has a different perspective. What you might think is a vindication of your program, your boss might see as a job that does not necessarily need to get done. The point is be prepared with a supportable reason or a significant result and you will go away the winner.

EFFECTIVENESS: WAS THE PROBLEM SOLVED?

It is possible to calculate the percent of effectiveness by dividing the number of satisfactory resolutions by the total number of counseling sessions. The only problem is in reaching agreement on what is a satisfactory resolution. Followup cannot be done on many issues because of their sensitive personal nature. You cannot ask employees if they are still mainlining drugs.

However, some cases are a little more obvious. Very often there is simply a question to be answered. Sometimes you can see for sure that you prevented an unwanted termination. If there is a conflict that has been resolved, that can be shown. When unproductive employees have their concerns taken care of and their productivity goes up, that is a measurable payoff. A rehabilitated alcoholic is an obvious result of professional help. The policy and procedures training program mentioned before is a very visible example. There are some instances wherein you can show unequivocably that counseling paid off. Reductions in turnover and absenteeism or increases in productivity are measurable results. However, much of the work of a counselor will have to be assessed by word-of-mouth reports, which is all right. If you can show that you have had a number of success stories, you do not have to quantitatively evaluate everything you did in employee relations.

A QUARTERLY VIEW

Financial reporting is typified by reports of earnings for the present quarter versus the same quarter a year previous. This approach can be applied in human resources as well. One place where it fits is with counseling. Figure 11.4 shows a quarter by quarter comparison of counseling by topic, giving both the number of contacts and the total time. The example shown would be a year-end review. From it one could look for seasonal trends which predict probable occurrences. In the sample, the third quarter appears to be a time when there are less problems than at others. This means a slackening of the workload and a time when other types of activities might be planned.

The point of this kind of reporting is that it helps the employee relations manager plan and organize the staff for maximum performance. Good managers plan ahead, but that is hard to do when you have only a hazy notion of what to expect. A detailed knowledge of what has gone before is invaluable for planning the future.

	Q1		Q2		Q3		Q4	
	1980 #/hr	1981 #/hr	1980 #/hr	1981 #/hr	1980 #/hr	1981 #/hr	1980 #/hr	1981 #/hr
Policies and procedures	186/34	114/46.5	158/48.9	129/39.6	145/36.9	66/17.1	186/37.3	89/31.3
Employee performance problems	179/62	105/53.1	138/48.2	144/61.5	120/40	113/41.1	143/58	135/62.8
Personal problems	68/39.2	186/78.8	192/56.2	84/58.8	81/52.3	72/28.2	114/49	114/61.6
Job performance problems	68/31.2	99/51.6	149/64	63/42	116/43	84/28.4	111/46.1	92/48.5
Salary administration	44/24	0	37/15.1	0	33/14.8	1/0.3	38/17.9	4/2.5
EEO matters	4/1	21/24.9	5/2.6	3/1.5	22/12.9	6/2	10/5.5	4/2.3
Exit interviews	114/44.6	81/32.4	134/56	91/32.1	118/58.6	186/41	122/53	64/29.3
Career opportunities program	17/5.9	284/71.1	33/10.8	258/94.8	15/5.1	217/53.1	21/7.3	136/69.6
Career pathing	26/15.9	42/22.5	18/3.3	15/12	6/2	35/16	14/7	118/55
Management training	0	27/21	0	291/219	0	57/39.4	0	0
Employee training	0	12/12	0	45/72	0	6/3.8	0	13/26.8
Termination procedure	68/11.1	0	58/20.6	0	61/19.2	0	62/16.9	0
Total	758/268	813/406	906/318	1116/633	717/285	764/270	741/290	761/390

Figure 11.4 Counseling Quarterly Report (Headquarters)

The Hidden Costs of Lost Time

ABSENCE

Employee absence is more than a nuisance; it is costly. If left unattended, absence can become a significant expense. There are many reasons for an employee to be absent from work. Some are legitimate. Sickness, family emergencies, or personal business that can be dealt with only during working hours are absences for which an employee reasonably takes a day of leave. However, there are other more capricious sources of absence, many of which can be prevented.

Survey data often shows a correlation between absence and dissatisfaction with pay. It is the employee's way of "getting even." The rationale used is, "you won't pay me what I am worth so I'll just take a day off and let you give me sick pay instead." Other sources of irritation and stress can also prompt an absence. Poor supervisory practices most often correlate with turnover, but they may also foster absence. Excessive workloads for a long period of time can cause a minor psychological or physical breakdown resulting in a couple of days off. In the worst cases, high stress can cause permanent problems. However the absence comes about, there are several ways to measure its rate of occurrence and its cost to the organization.

The basic absence rate calculation used in most national surveys, such as the ASPA-BNA, is shown in Formula ER–7.

Absence Rate

$$AR = \frac{WDL}{e \times WD} \qquad (ER-7)$$

where   AR = absence rate
   WDL = worker days lost through absence (e.g., 400)
      e = average employee population (e.g., 550)
   WD = number of work days available per employee (e.g., 22)

EXAMPLE

$$AR = \frac{400}{550 \times 22}$$
$$= \frac{400}{12,100}$$
$$= 3.3\%$$

As with most other ratios, this one can be computed by department to find locations where absence levels are relatively high. It can also be applied to job groups to search out types of employees who are exceedingly absent. In order for an absence control program to work there are two prerequisites: accurate employee time records and a standard acceptable absence rate.

Knowing the amount of time lost through absence is the starting point. The other issue is the hidden cost of absence. Kuzmits[3] provided the basis for the formula used to measure absenteeism costs, as shown in Formula ER-8.

Absenteeism Cost

$$AC/E = \frac{ML(Wh + EBC) + S(R/h + SBC) + Misc}{E} \qquad (ER-8)$$

where   AC/E = absence cost per employee
     ML = total work hours lost for all reasons except holidays and vacations (e.g., 78,336)
     Wh = weighted average hourly pay level for groups (e.g., 85% of hourly absences at \$6.25 = \$5.31; 13% of nonexempt absences at \$5.95 = \$0.77; 2% of exempt absences at \$12.45 = \$0.25; total = \$6.33)
   EBC = cost of employee benefits (e.g., 35% of pay: \$6.33 × 35% = \$2.22)
      S = supervisory hours lost due to employee absence, based on sampling to estimate average hours per day

spent dealing with problems resulting from absences: production rescheduling, instructing replacements, counseling and disciplining absentees (e.g., ½ hour per day = 3840)

R/h = average hourly pay for supervisors (e.g., $7.25)

SBC = cost of supervisor's benefits (e.g., 35% of $7.25 = $2.54)

Misc = other costs, temporary help, overtime, production losses, machine downtime, quality problems (e.g., $38,500)

E = total employees (e.g., 1200)

EXAMPLE

$$AC = \frac{(78{,}336 \times \$8.55) + (3840 \times \$9.79) + \$38{,}500}{1200}$$

$$= \frac{\$669{,}773 + \$37{,}594 + \$38{,}500}{1200}$$

$$= \frac{\$745{,}867}{1200}$$

$$= \$621.56$$

Measuring this quantity brings home to supervisors and managers that absence carries with it a high hidden cost. The peripheral costs of supervisory time, temporary help, poor quality work, and so on add significantly to the loss. Still another way of viewing absence is from the standpoint of its effect on labor utilization. This can be seen in the two-step process of Formula ER–9.

Effect of Absenteeism on Labor Utilization

$$U = \frac{Nh}{h} \tag{ER–9}$$

where U = labor utilization percentage

Nh = nonproductive hours: absence, breaks, downtime, prep time, rework (e.g., 380 hours)

h = work hours available (e.g., 10 employees $\times$ 40 hours $\times$ 4 weeks = 1600 hours)

EXAMPLE

$$U = \frac{380}{1600}$$

$$= 24\% \text{ (utilization} = 76\%)$$

To show the effect of absenteeism, subtract absent hours (e.g., 80) from Nh and recompute.

EXAMPLE

$$U = \frac{380 - 80}{1600}$$
$$= \frac{300}{1600}$$
$$= 19\% \text{ (utilization} = 81\%)$$

Utilization would have been 5 percent higher if no employees had been absent.

Absence is an insidious type of problem because it is, by definition, invisible. It is not so obviously a matter of something going wrong as it is a case of something that should occur not occurring. The missing occurrence is the arrival of the scheduled employee at work. When that does not happen it sets in motion a chain of other events which negatively impact hard measures like quality and productivity.

VALUE OF ABSENCE CONTROL

Absenteeism may also affect things such as morale for the employees who come to work every day. It can create other types of dissatisfaction among employees in a work group, who may have to take time to indoctrinate temporary employees filling in for those who are frequently absent. By maintaining current data on absence and showing its negative effects, you may cause management to step up to an issue they would rather ignore. If they do you will have helped them save the company money and improve morale.

Most surveys have shown that Pareto's law applies to absences; that is, approximately 20 percent of the employees account for 80 percent of the absences. If we were to divide all absence into three types we could label them capricious, personal business, and problem. The first category I mentioned before. It covers the days off people take because they are angry with the company or are not motivated to work that day. The first sunny day in spring, the opening of hunting season, or the morning-after blues are examples of no work motivation. Personal business is just what it implies. Sometimes a person has to take care of family matters and they can do that only during working hours. Going to a lawyer, closing the sale or purchase of a house, picking up grandma at the airport, and taking a child to the doctor or on a special shopping trip are a few of the many responsibilities which we all have. Employees

Category	Number of employees	Average days lost previous	Total days lost	Total estimated cost, in dollars
Alcohol	25	20	500	34,545
Drugs	8	28	224	15,746
Family	21	15	315	21,763
Mental	6	24	144	9,948
Other	9	12	108	7,461
Total	69	19.8	1291	89,193

Figure 12.1 Frequency of Absence by Category

figure that if they have a lot of sick leave earned they may as well use some of that rather than take a vacation day. The last category, problem, covers the gut-wrenching matters of alcohol and drug abuse, and mental health and family problems. Sooner or later, these issues show up at the employee relations office. We have even created a special service to help employees deal with these concerns. We call them employee assistance (EA) programs. If you check the work records of employees who utilize the EA programs, you will probably find that they have higher than average rates of absenteeism. Figure 12.1 shows a typical example.

By computing the lost time costs you can find the effect of absenteeism on your organization's profit and loss statement. If you are able to "solve" some of these problems through your EA service, you can track the effect that it has on absenteeism. If it reduces absences, which it will, calculate the cost saving to the company. This can be expressed in terms of productive days gained and the dollar value of that gain. You may find that the EA program more than pays for itself in direct benefits. The rehabilitation of a sick employee or the rescue of a troubled family is an added incalculable payoff.

In conclusion, absence affects both the hard data issues of productivity as well as human issues, such as morale. Excessively absent workers impact the morale of the employees who come to work every day and can create other types of dissatisfaction among their coworkers. By maintaining current data on absence and showing its negative effects you may cause management to step up to an issue they sometimes ignore. If they do, you will have helped them save the company money and improve morale.

CLARIFYING THE CONCEPT OF TURNOVER

Movement of employees into and out of organizations, commonly called *turnover,* is one of the more heavily studied organizational phenomena. The U.S. Bureau of Labor Statistics uses the terms *accessions* and *separations* to describe movements across organizational boundaries. Transfers and promotions are not considered part of turnover because they do not involve movement across the membership boundary of an organization. Accessions are generally *new hires.* Separations are subdivided into *quits, layoffs,* and *discharges.* Turnover is further typed as *voluntary* and *involuntary.* Quits (and resignations) are the normal label for voluntary departures. Involuntary examples are dismissals (firings), layoffs, retirements, and deaths. Under normal business conditions voluntary turnover is greater than involuntary. Voluntary is more often studied by management due to its desire to reduce it or maintain it at an acceptable level.

Zero turnover is not desirable for several reasons. First, long-tenured employees generally have higher salaries. If all employees stayed and the organization grew at a normal rate, most employees would soon be at or near the top of their pay ranges and total salary expense would be very high. Second, new employees bring new ideas. A number of stagnant organizations have inbred and are no longer in touch with their constituency. The automobile industry lost touch with its public in the 1960s and allowed foreign car manufacturers to take as much as 50 percent of some U.S. car markets. Labor unions have, in some cases, lost contact and control of their membership. While failing to seek out new leadership from the rank and file, labor leaders continued to champion the initial causes of the labor movement. In the 1970s they awakened to find that the membership had new needs and new values. Any organization must continually renew itself with fresh ideas from new members. Therefore, a small amount of turnover is healthy.*

Rather than focus on the causes of turnover we will concentrate on methods of analysis. The question "what is the turnover percentage in your organization?" is too simplistic. A single number tells little. Even if the number compares favorably with a previous period, it is not very helpful. One number does not tell who is leaving or for what reasons. As with most variables we have discussed, the data has to be cut into smaller, more homogeneous clusters if it is to yield true understanding of the phenomena at work.

The two basic calculations from which all subdivisions are made are the accession rate and the separation rate. They are shown in Formulas ER–10 and ER–11.

---

*Readers who are deeply interested in the subject of turnover should consult the excellent text by James Price.[4] Many of Price's concepts have been incorporated into this chapter.

Accession Rate

$$AR = \frac{H}{e} \hspace{3cm} \text{(ER–10)}$$

Separation Rate

$$SR = \frac{NT}{e} \hspace{3cm} \text{(ER–11)}$$

where　AR = accession rate
　　　　SR = separation rate
　　　　H = number hired during the period (e.g., 725)
　　　NT = number terminated during the period (e.g., 656)
　　　　e = average employee population (e.g., 3097)

EXAMPLE

$$AR = \frac{725}{3097} \hspace{1cm} SR = \frac{656}{3097}$$
$$= 23.4\% \hspace{1.5cm} = 21.2\%$$

For many years there was little agreement on the employee population figure that should be used. Some practitioners used beginning of period population and others used average or end of period population as the divisor. Within the past couple of years a standard, *average population,* seems to be developing. This factors out most of the effects of heavy hiring or terminating.

SUBDIVIDING FOR UNDERSTANDING

There is practically no end to the ways in which turnover data can be cut. Some common categories are

- Length of service of current employees
- Length of service of terminating employees
- Stability (instability) factor of a given population
- Survival (loss) rate of new hires
- Termination rate by organizational unit (department, headquarters, division)
- Termination rate by demographic group (age, race, sex, education, grade, performance level, job classification)
- Termination rate by reason for leaving

The formulas are all quite similar. Except for length of service, it is only a matter of dividing the number of employees in the referent group by the average population.

Tenure or length of service is computed in Formulas ER–12 and ER–13.

Average Tenure—Current Employees

$$SS = \frac{TSS}{E} \tag{ER–12}$$

Exemployees Average Service Period

$$SL = \frac{TSL}{E} \tag{ER–13}$$

where   SS = average length of service of current employees—stayers

       TSS = total sum of years of service of all staying employees (e.g., 112,025)

       SL = average length of service of departed employees—leavers

       TSL = total sum of years of service of all departed employees (e.g., 16,589)

       E = total number of employees in that group (e.g., stayers = 2041; leavers = 1056)

EXAMPLE

$$SS = \frac{112,025}{2041} \qquad SL = \frac{16,589}{1056}$$

$$= 5.5 \text{ years} \qquad = 1.6 \text{ years}$$

This calculation suggests that most employees who leave have relatively short tenure with the organization. We know from experience that the longer employees stay with an organization, the more likely they are to continue to stay. Another way to put it is that most of the turnover comes in the first 2 years of service.

One way to periodically check the preceding assumption is to compute stability factors. These calculations tell you whether or not the turnover rate for a given population, i.e., employees with 5+ years of service, is changing. It answers questions like, "are our older employees leaving at the same rate as we would expect them to?" You can calculate it from either side: stability or instability, as shown in Formulas ER–14 and ER–15.

Stability Factor

$$SF = \frac{OS}{E} \tag{ER–14}$$

Instability Factor

$$IF = \frac{OL}{E} \qquad (ER–15)$$

where   SF = stability factor of an existing population

         OS = original employees who remain for the period, for example, 1 year (e.g., 832)

         IF = instability factor of an existing population

        OL = original employees who left during the period (e.g., 80)

         E = employee population at the beginning of the period (e.g., 912)

EXAMPLE

$$SF = \frac{832}{912} \qquad IF = \frac{80}{912}$$
$$= 91.2\% \qquad = 8.8\%$$

Obviously, SF and IF are reciprocals. In this case, 91.2 percent of the employees with 5+ years of service stayed and 8.8 percent left during the past year. That can be compared with previous experience and a value judgment can be made.

Survival or loss rate of new hires is conceptually identical to stability factor, only here the base population is new hires and not existing employee groups. A time period, say a month or a quarter, is defined and all hires during that period are counted. At some point in the future, perhaps 6 months or 1 year later, all hires from the base period are traced and counted, either as stayers or as leavers. The computation is shown in Formulas ER–16 and ER–17.

Survivor Rate

$$SR = \frac{HS}{H} \qquad (ER–16)$$

Loss Rate

$$LR = \frac{HL}{H} \qquad (ER–17)$$

where   SR = survival rate of new hires

        HS = number of new hires from the period who are still employed, stayers (e.g., 209)

        LR = wastage or loss rate

        HL = number of new hires who left, leavers (e.g., 79)

         H = total number of new hires during the period (e.g., 288)

EXAMPLE

$$SR = \frac{209}{288} \qquad LR = \frac{79}{288}$$
$$= 72.6\% \qquad = 27.4\%$$

This measure can be used as part of the recruiter effectiveness composite. However, since a new hire's survival is out of the hands of the recruiter, remember to use this indicator with great caution.

MULTIDIMENSIONAL ANALYSIS

It is often enlightening to look at turnover from more than one perspective at a time. For instance, you could correlate turnover data by age and level of performance. First, you could compute the percentage of turnover for age groups (e.g., 20 to 24, 26 to 29, 30 to 34, etc.). Then, you could do the same for levels of performance. There are two ways to look at performance, as shown in Formula ER–18.

Turnover/Performance Relationships

$$PT = \frac{R}{L} \qquad PT = \frac{R}{TR} \tag{ER–18}$$

where   PT = percent terminating at each performance level
         R = number rated at each level
         L = total number terminated
       TR = total rated at a given level

EXAMPLES

$$PT = \frac{27}{225} = 12.0\% \quad \text{or} \quad \frac{27}{79} = 34.2\% \quad \text{performance level 6}$$

$$= \frac{79}{225} = 35.1\% \quad \text{or} \quad \frac{79}{365} = 21.6\% \quad \text{performance level 5}$$

$$= \frac{63}{225} = 28.0\% \quad \text{or} \quad \frac{63}{593} = 10.6\% \quad \text{performance level 4}$$

$$= \frac{42}{225} = 18.7\% \quad \text{or} \quad \frac{42}{53} = 79.2\% \quad \text{performance level 3}$$

$$= \frac{8}{225^*} = 3.6\% \quad \text{or} \quad \frac{8}{10^*} = 80.0\% \quad \text{performance level 2}$$

In the sample, 225 employees were terminated. Twenty-seven were rated 6, or the highest level in their performance. In the total organization, 79 were rated 6. Thus, while 12 percent of the terminations came

*Column adds to 219 + 6 who did not get rated.

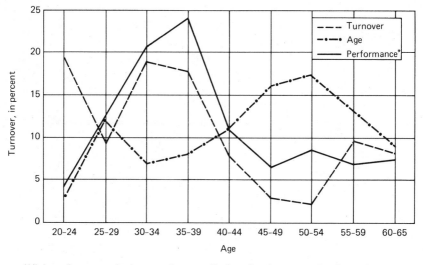

*High performers only: i.e., employees with 5 or 6 ratings on a 6-point scale.

Figure 12.2   Age-Performance-Turnover Relationship

from level 6, 34.2 percent of the organization's highest performers left. An additional measure which can be obtained is the performance level of the average terminee. This can be obtained through a weighted average calculation of the left column. The answer in this sample is 4.27. In order to correlate age, performance, and turnover you need to have both the age and performance rating of each terminee.

When you have the three types of data you can plot them all on a line chart. In the sample in Fig. 12.2 we are interested only in high performers. They are defined here as employees with performance ratings of 5 or 6 on the 6-point scale. Employees with ratings of 1 to 4 are not included.

This example shows an organization with some problems. You can no doubt see that turnover is highest from about age 27 to 38, which is also the age group that has a large percentage of high performers. In addition, as age increases the percent who are high performers decreases. The age profile shows a very large group in the 45 to 54 range. If you put some of these findings together you can see that there is reason for concern across all three dimensions. Multidimensional analysis is the best way to get inside the numbers to find correlations which point to otherwise invisible organizational phenomena.

Before we leave this area, a word needs to be said about looking at the reason for leaving. Most organizations collect data at termination time regarding the reason for the termination. If they do a good job of it, the data can be considered reliable. This information can be displayed very effectively in a multilevel bar chart similar to the one used

Direct Hiring Costs

New Hires

1. Advertising $ _____

2. Agency and search fees _____

3. Internal referral bonuses _____

4. Applicant expenses _____

5. Relocation expenses _____

6. Salary and benefits of staff _____

7. Employment office overhead _____

8. Recruiter's expenses _____

9. Total direct hiring costs _____

10. Divide line 9 by number hired. Cost per hire _____

Indirect Hiring Costs

11. Management time per hire _____

12. Supervisor/lead time per hire _____

13. Orientation and training per hire _____

14. Learning curve productivity loss or opportunity loss per hire _____

15. Total indirect hiring costs per hire _____

16. Total hiring costs per hire _____

17. Multiply line 16 by number hired Total hiring costs _____

Direct Internal Replacement Costs

Replacements

18. Applicant expenses $ _____

19. Relocation expenses _____

Direct Internal Replacement Costs (Continued)

Replacements (continued)

20. Salaries and benefits of staff $ _____

21. Employment office overhead   _____

22. Total direct replacement costs   _____

23. Divide line 22 by number placed.
Direct costs per placement   _____

Indirect Internal Replacement Costs

24. Management/time per hire   _____

25. Supervisor/lead interview time per hire   _____

26. Training time per hire   _____

27. Learning curve productivity loss or
opportunity loss per hire   _____

28. Total indirect replacement costs
per placement $ _____

29. Add lines 23 and 28. Total cost
per placement   _____

30. Multiply line 29 by number placed
Total internal replacement costs   _____

31. Total turnover costs   _____

32. Target percentage reduction   _____%

33. Potential savings $ _____

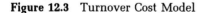

Figure 12.3 Turnover Cost Model

in the counseling area. It can also be displayed in a bar chart with an individual bar for each reason. All the other formulas we have looked at tell us who is leaving—this tells us why. Unless you know the why you cannot do much about the who. After you know why, you can figure out what to do and where to do it. That kind of analysis and action is bound to produce positive results.

TURNOVER COST

Everyone knows that turnover is costly. Just how much it costs depends on what you include. Expenses generally fall into categories: employment costs, training and orientation costs, and lost productivity or opportunity costs. It is impossible to calculate exactly what all that amounts to, but it is substantial. Probably the most practical and comprehensive cost estimation model is Hall's.[5] While formidable in appearance, it is simple to understand and use. The model shown in Fig. 12.3 is derived from Hall's work.

UNEMPLOYMENT CLAIMS CONTROL

An important but seldom seen activity is supervision of the unemployment insurance claim process. In most states when an applicant's claim for unemployment benefits is denied this reflects favorably on the employer's experience rating. Accordingly, it behooves the company to contest all claims from former employees which it believes are unfounded. Often this task is the responsibility of the employee relations group. A simple but effective way to report the results of that cost containment effort is shown in Fig. 12.4.

Note first that the savings from the two previous years is shown in the upper right corner. This serves two purposes: one is public relations and the other is motivational. First, assuming this is a report which is updated monthly and distributed outside your department, the report continually reminds the executive reader that you are cognizant of the value of cost containment. It does not take long using this reporting philosophy to convince line management that you are an integral part of the profit team and not just a cost center. Second, keeping past performance visible for your employee relations staff helps to stimulate them to do better. I remember vividly how a determined employee relations manager reacted when I told her that I thought we could save an additional 25 percent in the coming year. I thought it was a formidable goal; one that I would have trouble selling to her. She looked at the report and saw how well she had done for the past 2 years. Then she looked down the savings column for the current year, month by month. For a long minute she sat there and I could see the wheels turning in her head. Finally, she looked up and said, "we can do it!" She knew from looking at her past performance, exceptional as it already was, that she could try a new or better technique and meet the objective. I am convinced that without the past record of success to convince her she would have been reluctant to commit herself.

| 1980 Year-end total | | | | | | 68,835.00 |
| 1981 Year-end total | | | | | | 128,227.60 |

1982	New claims contested	Determinations		Appeals		Pending	Potential savings, in dollars
		Won	Lost	Won	Lost		
Jan	15	3	0	0	0	12	4,873.00
Feb	16	2	5	1	0	21	4,680.00
Mar	15	2	5	0	0	29	4,810.00
Apr	10	1	1	0	0	37	2,912.00
May	20	2	0	0	0	55	4,602.00
Jun	18	12	7	0	1	54	32,162.00
Jul	9	5	1	1	0	57	13,754.00
Aug	16	6	2	1	1	65	17,030.00
Sep	15	6	3	1	0	71	20,020.00
Oct	19	7	6	2	0	77	20,098.00
Nov	10	4	6	0	0	77	9,906.00
Dec	8	10	5	2	0	70	26,314.00
1982 Totals	171	60	41	8	2	70	163,161.00

Figure 12.4   Unemployment Insurance Record

One of the great unseen benefits of measurement is motivation. When your people see that they can do something and do it well, they are motivated to surpass themselves. There is a cycle to high performance that is based on the principles inherent in self-esteem. In order for a person to build and maintain high self-esteem they must be successful. By starting with reasonable, attainable goals and achieving them, the person feels a sense of increased self-esteem. This motivates him or her to try for a higher goal. If that is challenging but possible the chances are that it will be reached. Success once again increases self-confidence and self-esteem and the upward spiral continues. Everyone wins, the person grows, the department succeeds, and the organization prospers.

SUMMARY

Absenteeism, turnover, and unemployment claims offer the human resources professional an excellent arena in which to exercise analytic and creative skills to obtain visible results. Everyone can appreciate the value of reduced absence and turnover and controlled unemployment claims. Best of all, from your standpoint, the results are very quantifiable. You will be able to show management exactly how you are contributing to the bottom line.

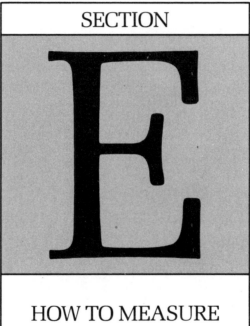

SECTION

E

HOW TO MEASURE
TRAINING
AND DEVELOPMENT

Career Development

DEVELOPMENT IS MORE THAN TRAINING

Employee development is usually approached one of two ways: from the viewpoint of the job or from the viewpoint of the employee. Either we try to fit people to the job or the job to people. Each approach has value. In entry-level jobs there is normally little freedom of choice for the employee. The task is very specific and the steps to its accomplishment thoroughly routinized. However, as you proceed up the job ladder to higher-level positions and into supervisory and managerial ranks, more creativity and individual style is allowed. For the sake of space, this discussion will confine itself to supervisory levels and above. It does not exclude nonmanagerial jobs. The premise and procedure apply to professional level, individual contributor positions as well.

The professional football team the Raiders have operated under the philosophy, "find an exceptional athlete and teach him to play the position that best utilizes his talents." This approach has worked very well for them. For the period 1963 to 1982 they have the best won-lost record in the league. Business organizations often do that in their college recruitment programs. Since the young person has little or no relevant work history, it makes sense to look for the broadest range of potential possible, with the knowledge that a large organization can always find a place to employ people with exceptional aptitudes. However, as applicants for middle- and upper-level positions are reviewed the organization asks itself how this person will fill a given job. It is my belief that good athletes can play a number of positions, but not any position. Likewise, talented people can do several jobs well, but not every job. Practically speaking, we are all somewhat limited by our aptitudes. I know personally that there are a number of jobs that I can do, but there are a larger number that I cannot do well. I think this is true for most people. The most effective development approach probably combines elements of both the job perspective and the human perspective.

My contact with organizational training over more than 15 years makes me believe that professional and managerial training takes place in a partial vacuum. Much of it is program driven, rather than objective driven. By this I mean that many training programs are designed and conducted with no specific goal in view. Many times I have been approached by senior management to conduct a program. When I ask why they want it the reasons are vague, illogical, or basically nonexistent. "Because XYZ Corporation is doing it" is not what I call a reason. "Because we want to show employees we are interested in them" is equally inadequate. I suppose there may be room for general information training, but from a priority standpoint there are many more immediate specific needs. In the following pages I would like to suggest a methodology which is logical, specific, measurable in terms of results, and much more efficient than the current standard approach.

TARGET TRAINING

The most common stimulus for the creation of a training program is a needs analysis. These surveys ask people to give the training department information on the skills that are needed in the organization. The resulting data is generally a collection of unsubstantiated opinions about a broad range of issues that can be fitted into a formal educational experience, i.e., a class. Based on this response, organizations will develop a curriculum of perhaps a dozen or more programs. These will subsequently be offered and conducted, and perhaps some self-report type of evaluation will be carried out. The cost of these procedures often runs into the millions of dollars, and when they are over no one asks what the return on that investment was? Without belaboring the unbusinesslike nature of that type of system, let me suggest what may not be perfect, but is certainly more reasonable.

The place to start is with the creation of your development team. Because employee development is a complex art several disciplines must play a role. I believe there are at least six types of people who are needed. First, a line management representative must be included from the area you plan on servicing. After all, development of employees is a manager's job, and the training department is just there to support the effort. Next, you will need representation from human resources planning, staffing, and career development. The planners should have a unique perspective because they are closer to the corporate business plan than anyone within human resources development. Their job is to see that the business plan is translated into an HR department plan. Staffing is involved because they are the ones who have to find the people who will later be developed. Career development people are, in my scheme, the ones who design career path systems, do career counseling and assessment, and handle the job-posting program. I believe job posting is more effective when run as a career development system rather than as an adjunct to employment. Job posting, beyond just filling vacancies, is an attempt to develop people by moving them into jobs which they are interested in doing and which suit their skills. The last groups to be involved on the development team are the trainers—management development and organization development professionals. They are the ones who ultimately will have to design the formal and informal development experiences. Each of the functions represented on this team brings with it a unique viewpoint and a special set of skills and knowledge. Cumulatively, they should be able to select and design the most effective program in the most efficient manner.

Once the team is formed a target development area is selected. There are many ways this can be done and I will not go into all the alternatives here. For the sake of example, let us say that it has been decided that one of the areas which most needs development is the customer service managers (CSM). In order to match and develop people for that job we need to do two things. First, the job duties, responsibilities, and requisite skills and knowledge have to be defined. A thorough job description usually provides most of that data, and it can be augmented with whatever else is needed.

Second, a model of an effective customer service manager needs to be developed. There are many methods for doing this, examples of which can be found in career development textbooks. Fundamentally, the model describes the behavior and the results obtained by an effective manager. The data is drawn from records and interviews within the customer service department and from contacts with people who interface with the department. The result of this two-pronged approach is a clear picture of what you are trying to find and develop in potential managers. There are selection methods, such as assessment programs and testing, which will surface the people who have the best potential for being a successful CSM. These people should be the first to be developed. We are in the business of helping people grow and succeed, and this method offers them an excellent chance to do so. How well they do can be tracked and compared to the traditional hit and miss method. The results should show that the resources which were put to this program generated a favorable return on investment.

JOB POSTING AS CAREER DEVELOPMENT

Earlier I alluded to the idea that a posting system is a career development activity. Whether or not you agree with that, you can still measure the relationships of the job-posting system to the development of employees.

Mechanically, the posting process works like the employment process. You produce applicants, make placements, and spend resources doing it. The first thing you can show management is the volume of applicants and placements handled each month. This type of data lends itself to bar charting. Each month you can draw in the bars representing the number of applicants and the number of placements. A quick visual survey tells the reader something about the trend in workloads as well as the results.

The second issue you can talk about is the cost per placement. In the employee relations section of this book you were shown how to calculate the cost of hire and cost of replacement from internal sources. Using those two figures you can demonstrate how much you save the organization on the average every time you fill a job through the

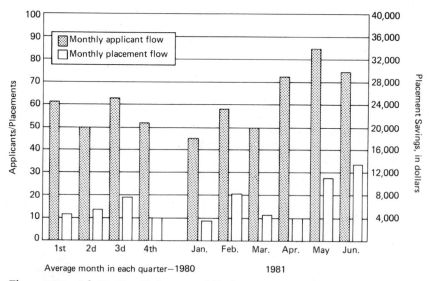

Figure 13.1   Job-Posting Volume and Savings

posting system. This number could be carried on one side of the monthly report. Shown on a cumulative cost savings bar, management could watch it grow each month. Figure 13.1 is an example of such a report. This data can be summarized on a quarterly basis and year-to-year comparisons can be made. By using the financial type of reporting, i.e., quarterlies with year-to-year comparisons, your documentation will begin to look more like standard business reports. This lends credibility to them and stimulates readership.

Management Development

EDUCATE OR TRAIN?

For people who are interested in measuring the results of their development programs there is a very fundamental, unavoidable question: "what is your overriding objective?" Do you want to educate people or do you want to train them? Education is the presentation of concepts and information to people for the purpose of imparting knowledge. Training is more of an interactive event whose goal is to make a person proficient. It is one thing to know; it is something different to be able to do.

In my experience I would speculate that at least 75 percent of the supervisory and management programs I have seen are primarily educational as opposed to training sessions. Most of the time is spent dealing with concepts of communication, motivation, leadership, and the like. The student-worker goes away better informed about these principles of management. Even when programs appear to deal with specifics they are still presented in an educational manner. A good example of this is a class in conflict resolution. These programs usually spend a good part of the time in the beginning covering the research findings which are the current theoretical basis of the topic. Then they turn to a case study or a game simulation so that the subject can be viewed in some kind of context. It is hoped that this exposure will give the student-worker a thorough understanding that can later be transferred to the work place.

That method is perfectly satisfactory if the objective is to educate someone. However, if you want to measure the result of your development effort at a level beyond attitude or knowledge it is impossible. It would be suspect, if not invalid, to infer that something happened in the work place as a result of a "training" experience if the program were conducted as described above. We cannot claim to have made someone proficient at something if we have presented only concepts.

Proficient is defined with one word—skilled. In order to become skilled you must have more than knowledge; you need to apply that information. If you wait for the employees to apply it on the job after the class is over, then they have trained themselves. You have educated them. Bottom line: cause and effect relationships cannot be proven in educational programs. In other words, if you educate, you cannot prove that your program was the causal force in the person's new behavior.

If you want to measure your results you must provide skill training. In order to do that you have to start at the beginning. As Bob Mager states,

> Before you prepare instruction, before you select procedures or subject matter or material, it is important to be able to state clearly just what you intend the results of that instruction to be.[1]

Mager goes on to point out that your instructional objective should state: 1) what you want the learner to be able to do, 2) under what conditions you want the learner to be able to do it, and 3) how well it must be done. If you do that at the beginning, then all design and delivery decisions are made under those criteria. In the end it is relatively easy to test for acquired skills. In addition, it is usually possible to go into the organization later to find out if the skills were used and what impact they had.

THREE BASIC MEASURES

When management takes an active interest in training it usually looks at cost first. They want to know how much was spent on training. The second question asked is, what did we teach the employees? Implied in that is the hopeful assumption that they learned something useful. The third, and least considered, issue is, did anything happen in the organization as a result of the training? Fortunately, if you design training programs along the line that Mager suggests, you will be able to answer those questions.

The three basic measures of training are cost, change, and impact.

- Cost—expense per unit of training delivered
- Change—gain (hopefully) in skill or knowledge or positive change in attitude by the trainee
- Impact—results or outcomes from the trainee's use of new skills, knowledge, or attitudes

We will examine each of these measures by using different analytic models to illustrate the many ways in which training and development can be quantitatively evaluated. As always, the issue is not can it be done, but what is the better way to do it?

Cost

This is the easiest variable to measure. So long as accurate accounting is maintained, cost measurement is simple. The simplest calculation is a matter of adding up all expenses and dividing the total by the number of people trained. Expenditure variables will differ depending on the number of direct and indirect costs included. Samples of direct costs are

- Consultant fees
- Training room rental (if offsite)
- Supplies
- Refreshments
- Travel and lodging

Examples of indirect costs would be mostly overhead types of factors such as

- Trainer's salaries and benefits
- Trainee's salaries and benefits
- Department overhead

Hence, the calculation for cost per trainee would be as shown in Formula D–1.

*Cost per Trainee**

$$C/T = \frac{CC + TR + S + RC + T\&L + TS + PS + OH}{PT} \tag{D-1}$$

*If you want to add in program development (PD) cost you would divide total PD cost by the number of people to be trained. Then add the pro rata result to the number in the example [$274.38].

where   C/T = cost per trainee
        CC = consultant costs (e.g., $2000)
        TR = training facility rental (e.g., $350)
         S = supplies, workbooks, paper, and pencils (e.g., $1100)
        RC = refreshments (e.g., $75)
       T&L = travel and lodging for trainees and trainers (e.g., $2400)
        TS = trainers' salary and benefits (e.g., $250)
        PS = participants' salary and benefits (e.g., $4300)
        OH = training department overhead (e.g., $500)
        PT = number of people trained (e.g., 40)

EXAMPLE

$$C/T = \frac{\$2000 + 350 + 1100 + 75 + 2400 + 250 + 4300 + 500}{40}$$

$$= \frac{\$10,975}{40}$$

$$= \$274.38$$

A very basic training program cost report would include variables such as

- Total training costs
- Total hours of instruction
- Total number of trainees
- Cost per trainee
- Cost per trainee hour

Cost per trainee hour is a finer and more valuable measure than cost per trainee. The use of hours serves to normalize or standardize the denominator across programs of differing lengths. The calculation for cost per trainee hour is shown in Formula D–2.

Cost per Trainee Hour

$$C/Th = \frac{TC}{PT \times Th} \tag{D–2}$$

where   C/Th = cost per trainee hour
         TC = total cost of training (e.g., $10,975)
         PT = number trained (e.g., 40)
         Th = hours of training (e.g., 16)

EXAMPLE

$$C/Th = \frac{\$10,975}{40 \times 16}$$
$$= \frac{10,975}{640}$$
$$= \$17.15$$

In addition to looking at the raw cost of a program you can do some comparison costing. That can be a comparison of training expenditures among various groups. You could check to see the amount of money being spent on exempt versus non-exempt employees. You could look at it across departments, EEO categories, or job groups. The purpose would be to make sure that you are training everyone to the necessary extent.

You can also compare program costs between internal and external sources. You will almost always find that it is cheaper to bring a program in-house than it is to send people to it. That is fine if you want to show management which is the less costly approach. However, be careful with this because there is more to training than cost. You may not be able to provide the same level of quality if you do it in-house. You or your staff instructor may not be as expert in the subject as the outside presenter. That problem is solved if you can hire the outside expert as a consultant to conduct the program. Still, there are other benefits from outside programs which cannot be matched. The opportunity to associate with people from other companies is often very valuable. Your trainee has a chance to pick up knowledge beyond what the trainer offers. Some people are sent away to programs as a reward or to give them a break from work. People even get sent to offsite programs to give their supervisor a break from them. Whatever the reason, offsite training may be the appropriate choice. However, if cost is the key consideration, you will always be able to show it is less expensive to do a program in-house. The main reason is that the fee per student will be lower if you have a group. Secondly, you won't have to spend as much for nontraining purposes such as travel, lodging, food, and sundry expenses.

The final cost issue that we will deal with before looking at one of the analytic models is the make-buy decision. The number one question underlying training is, "is it cheaper to train employees or to recruit them?" By now you have seen how to calculate employment, turnover, and training expenses. You will often find that it costs more to recruit people with certain skills that it does to train the existing staff. One benefit of training over recruiting is that your current employees are a known quantity. No matter how good the recruits look they are a question mark. You do not know how new people will fit with your employee group, the organizational philosophy, or the operating style. If you know the relative costs of the make-buy choice, your information should add value to the decision process.

Input Analysis

An input analysis approach is a systemic method of identifying and comparing the many costs involved in two or more training programs. It does this by breaking down the total training process into its main phases, which are then matrixed with the basic inputs. The matrix is shown in Fig. 14.1. Each cell is filled in with the appropriate cost figure, and all phases and inputs are totaled. One matrix is completed for each program under consideration. The final set of matrices are compared for cost differences. This supplies the answer to which program is more cost efficient, but it says nothing about which will be most effective. Whether or not a comparison is desired, every training program should be subjected to an input analysis.

Programs are the trainer's tool. You should know how much the tool is going to cost and how that cost breakdown looks before you start a program.

Change

While it is important to know how much you are spending to train, how the money is being used, and who is getting the training, it is probably more important to know what the result or outcome is. Change can be measured at the individual level in terms of knowledge,

	Inputs, in dollars				
	People	Material	Equipment	Facilities	Total
Diagnosis					
Design					
Development					
Delivery					
Evaluation					
Total					

Figure 14.1   Training Input Analysis

skill, or attitude improvement. Comparisons can be made across groups as well.

There are several levels of sophistication in training evaluation. As the degree of sophistication goes up, the value tends to go up with it. Examples of before and after measures, which quantify the results of a training program, are presented in Formulas D–3 through D–6.

Knowledge Change

$$KC = \frac{K_A}{K_B} \qquad (D-3)$$

where   KC $=$ knowledge change
   $K_A =$ knowledge level after training
   $K_B =$ knowledge level before training

This information can be obtained by pre- and post-testing. Scores can be obtained before and after each class or before and after the total program. It not only serves to demonstrate that people are learning what you want them to learn (i.e., the objectives of the course), but test results point out specifically what is not being learned. By reviewing the tests in class, the trainer has an opportunity to reinforce the learning. Formula D–4 gives a similar calculation for skill changes.

Skill (Behavior) Change

$$SC = \frac{S_A}{S_B} \qquad (D-4)$$

where   SC $=$ observable change in skills as a result of training
   $S_A =$ skill demonstrated after training by work output, critical incidents of interpersonal relations, or other observable phenomena
   $S_B =$ skill level existing previous to the training using the same criteria as above.

Data for this skill change ratio can be gathered through questionnaires, interviews, demonstrations, or observation with trainers, subordinates, peers, or supervisors. The key to obtaining something of value from this measurement is in being as specific as possible in describing the skills or behaviors to be evaluated.

Attitude Change

$$AC = \frac{A_A}{A_B} \qquad (D-5)$$

where AC = attitude change
A_A = attitude after training
A_B = attitude before training

If the objective is to go beyond knowledge or skill change to attitude change, the same pre- and post-testing method can be used. In this case, either a standard or a specially designed and validated attitude instrument would be used. Since attitudes are particularly vulnerable to influences in the environment, thought should be given to the timing of the posttest. Attitudes immediately after the training may be affected once the trainee reenters the work environment. The change may be either positive or negative, and in either case will confound the change attributable to the training. A posttest 6 months after the conclusion of training could tell how much change has been impacted by the environment.

If you find that the environment does not support the new attitudes, it does not make sense to continue to train. Unless you do posttesting, you will never know what happened.

Performance Change

$$PC = \frac{P_A}{P_B} \tag{D–6}$$

where PC = change in work performance as measured by the organization's performance appraisal system
P_A = latest review score from a performance appraisal conducted at least 90 days after the training
P_B = performance review score from the performance appraisal conducted prior to the training

In this case, since performance appraisal scales are usually small (e.g., 1 through 5 or 1 through 6), the difference in a single score may appear dramatic in terms of percentage change. Caution should be exercised in discussing an individual's performance change lest you be accused of overstatement. This measure takes on more meaning when a large number of appraisals are compared and consistently positive results appear.

A final word of warning. There may be a halo effect. That is, the supervisor knows the employee went through training and expects improved performance. If the supervisor is not careful, something that is not there may be inferred.

Impact

The difference between change and impact measurement is one of degree not type. Whereas change and cost are two distinctly different variables, change and impact are sequential measures along a continuum. The following are two examples which may help to draw the distinction.

A machine operator, Debra, is taught to run a cutting machine. At the end of the program Debra's skill and knowledge can be tested by a performance test. Let us say that before the class she could cut 80 units per hour. After the class a test shows that she could cut 100 units per hour. Clearly, the level of skill and knowledge changed in a positive direction—Debra is more efficient as a result of the training. Then if she goes to work and consistently averages 100 cuts per hour, the impact of the training is felt in the cost of goods manufactured. Assuming the reject and scrap rate is the same as before, Debra is now 25 percent more productive. The component cost of labor as an input to the cutting cost is thus reduced by 25 percent.

In a second example, a salesperson, Peter, is put through a sales training course. The purpose of the class is to teach salespeople how to close a sale. At the end of class a test of knowledge of the principles can be given and a simulated sales call can be practiced. If Peter performs according to the model being taught, you can claim a change in skill and knowledge compared to precourse tests. The record of his subsequent customer calls and sales can be kept. If the ratio of sales to calls goes up, that is the impact measurement. A cost-benefit analysis will show that as a result of the training, which cost X dollars, the company is now getting Y dollars of production from Peter. Presumably Y is greater than X and is also more than it was before the training.

Most measurements of training are relatively simple. Except when you are running an experimental/control group comparison, you can get along without fancy statistics. The key factors are the discipline necessary to make sure all the details are attended to and the accuracy of the data. Cost-benefit analysis is common sense. Add in all the costs and measure it against the payoffs. The benefits may be both quantitative and qualitative. Productivity measurement is a matter of comparing the cost of specific inputs to specific outputs. It is an idea similar to cost-benefit analysis, but it is usually applied to issues which are very specific, narrow in scope, and quantitative in nature.

LEVELS OF EVALUATION

There are several levels of sophistication in training evaluation. As the degree of sophistication goes up, the value tends to increase with it.

The first, most used, and lowest value method is the *trainee reaction survey,* also called the "smile sheet." The nickname comes from the notion that if the trainer smiles a lot, the trainee will give the program a good evaluation. Self-report data is very weak, yet it continues to be the most common method. The second and slightly more useful method is the knowledge test. This is usually a paper and pencil quiz which measures how much the trainee knows. It is given after the program, and there is no pretest against which to compare scores. Therefore, there is no proof that the trainee's knowledge level increased because of the program. The third level measures performance after the program. This is better than the second level because you look at the trainee's ability to perform, but still there is no comparative data. The fourth level measures performance before and after the program and includes a retention of followup check some months later. This is a strong measure and the first one where you can infer causal relationships from the training. The fifth and top level is the same as four except the control group is compared to the trainee group. The control group is very similar to the trainee group except that it does not get trained. If the trainees' performance improves and the control group's does not, it is reasonable to claim that the training was the primary cause—provided there were no other identifiable intervening events. This last level is a time-consuming exercise and is not often done in industry.

A TRAINING MEASUREMENT SYSTEM

Throughout the text I have repeatedly pointed out that effective measurements can be carried out by using simple models. Training is a good example of that premise. Training, probably more than any other function, has control over its environment. Trainers can close their doors and design their courses as they please. Once they have the trainees in the classroom the trainers are the boss. Trainers can set up any reasonable sequence of events and put the trainees through them. Given that type of power it follows that trainers can make some very definitive statements about their work. And they can support their claims.

The system which follows provides the trainer with the data to carry out an evaluation on the fourth level described previously. By adding a control group to the process an evaluation on the fifth level is possible.

1. Set behavioral objectives for the trainees. For each session (module) specify the desired behaviors, the conditions, and the criteria of performance.
2. Design the program to meet the objectives.

3. Collect baseline data from the trainee's department(s). The variables measured must be ones which relate to the upcoming training. (To have a fifth level evaluation, select a control group at this point and collect the same data.)

4. Conduct the training. Give pre- and post-tests of skills and knowledge (or attitudes if appropriate) at each session.

5. Approximately 60 to 90 days after the final session collect data comparable to step 3.

6. Compare the step 3 and step 5 data. This is the before and after course impact evaluation. It tells you if the class appeared to make a difference. Look for extraneous variables which may have affected the results. (Compare to the control group if you have one.)

7. Approximately 6 months after the last session have the trainees return for a refresher day. Give them a retention test before you start the review. This tests how much they remember 6 months after the event.

If you have carried out all the prescribed steps, I guarantee that you will be surprised at the results of steps 6 and 7. In 5 years of running this type of training the class average for the 6-month retention test was never below 86 percent, and the standard deviations were extremely low. Your people will learn, they will use, and they will retain.

MEASURES OF MANAGEMENT

In about 1977 a nationally recognized training "expert" stood before the audience at a training conference and declared that supervisory and management development programs could not be measured for their effects. And he was right! He was correct within the context of training as he saw it. What he was talking about was education, not training. He was referring to classes on communication, motivation, and leadership. So long as he viewed training as the presentation of principles and concepts he was 100 percent correct.

But you know different. You know you have to get off the abstract level and train managers how to do a number of tasks better. If you do that you will be able to measure their performance as well as the impact of that performance. You see, management is a concept, an abstraction. No one has ever seen anyone "manage." It is not a concrete, observable, discrete act, and therein lies its mystery. Concepts cannot be measured since they exist only in the mind. Ergo, management cannot be measured since measurement requires something concrete and capable of specificity.

The solution is relatively simple and is to be found in the problem itself. If concepts cannot be measured because they are nonspecific and nonobservable, then the answer to the problem is to reduce them to their discrete, observable components. This is the methodology which physical and social scientists have always used. In order to understand the whole, one starts by learning as much as possible about the parts.

The same approach, much less demanding thankfully, can be used to understand more precisely what management is. Once we break down the process of management into a manager's many observable acts, the mystique disappears. Therefore, the real question is not, "what is management?" It is, "what do managers do?" The answer to this tells us what we can train and what we can measure.

We can show that managers perform management tasks better after a training program. They interview more efficiently, and they handle performance reviews and administer salaries with fewer problems. They coach, counsel, and discipline better. They budget more accurately, write more effectively, and schedule more efficiently. In short, they do the multitude of trainable tasks better.

As helpful and enlightening as that may be, it is still only part of the picture. Ultimately, a manager is measured by the results of the department. Results are a reflection of the manager's ability to direct human, financial, and technological resources to achieve the department's objectives. If we can find connections between the tasks a manager performs and the output of the department, we can show that improved task performance relates to department results. The connections are these. The tasks are the contexts within which one communicates, motivates, and leads. It is by improving task performance that we can help managers become better communicators, motivators, and leaders. Then, presuming management theory is correct, effective managers are good communicators, motivators, and leaders. And finally, effective managers are people who get results through other people.

Hopefully, this trip up and down the ladder of abstraction has demonstrated that you can infer that your training programs make effective managers if you can prove that you have helped them to perform their tasks better. And you can prove that if you follow a training system similar to the one outlined in this chapter.

CHAPTER 15

Organization Development

DOES ORGANIZATION DEVELOPMENT
HAVE A FUTURE?

The basic question which faces the organization development (OD) community is not, "what is the newest or best technique?" It is, "can OD be practiced so that it can prove that through its efforts organizational health and effectiveness were visibly improved?" If the answer to this is no, then I believe there is little chance that OD will have a long-term, meaningful role in business organizations.

Although management is generally becoming more enlightened about the treatment of workers, it is also becoming more demanding about the return on its investment. As I pointed out in the beginning of this book, markets are becoming more competitive and American business has no choice but to become more productive and efficient if it wants to prosper. It is not that executives do not appreciate the value of a high-quality working environment. In order for them to create an arena in which workers can self-actualize there must first be sufficient profit in the business to ensure its survival.

I believe that OD can prove its contribution. That is, it can measure its outcomes in quantitative as well as qualitative terms. The issue which has blocked measurement efforts up to now is not the mechanics of mathematics or experimentation, but an unwillingness to attempt measurement. Many OD professionals view themselves as being somehow related to the education and healing professions. And they simply cannot emotionally identify with quantitative analysis of their work.

199

To show how OD can be quantified without violating a sacred oath, it is necessary to examine three basic issues. This review will take us back to the early days of the discipline to look at how it viewed itself in terms of the definition of an organization.

ORGANIZATION DEVELOPMENT AND THE ORGANIZATION

Edgar Schein, one of the fathers of OD, provides a workable definition of an organization.

> The rational coordination of the activities of a number of people for the achievement of some common explicit purpose or goal, through division of labor and function, and through a hierarchy of authority and responsibility.[2]

The key words in that definition are people, activities, and achievement. These variables are all measurable at one level or another. To find out how, you have to look at the organization as a system.

The organization is viewed by OD as an open system which is characterized by inputs, processes, and outputs. It exists within a larger environment. It draws resources from that environment, processes them, and returns them in a changed and value-added form. Within itself, the organization has smaller systems which act in the same manner. They draw resources from the environment and from other subsystems, process them, and pass them on in an improved form. Hence, the idea of the organizational system has these characteristics: interaction and interdependence of elements, plus the goal of creating value-added outputs. To see how this relates to OD work, we must seek a definition of organization development.

There are many descriptions of what OD is. Fortunately, they all say pretty much the same thing. Richard Beckhard offered one which I have always felt was both comprehensive and efficient.

> Organization development is an effort 1) planned, 2) organization-wide, and 3) managed from the top, to 4) increase organization effectiveness and health through 5) planned interventions in the organization's processes, using behavioral science knowledge.[3]

Note that the goals are to increase organizational effectiveness and health. The issue of health is concerned with individuals' feelings and with interpersonal and group relationships. OD's assumption is that by improving individual work-related health the person will become more effective on the job. This should then lead to greater organizational effectiveness and profitability.

In summary, an organization is a collection of people, activities, and objectives. It is characterized by inputs, processes, and outputs which add value. OD is a planned intervention aimed at improving individual and organizational health and effectiveness. As far as I can see, there is nothing in those statements which prohibits quantitative evaluation.

WHY ORGANIZATION DEVELOPMENT IS NOT QUANTITATIVELY EVALUATED

Since measurement is clearly possible, why is it seldom attempted? There are several reasons. They are very similar to the excuses given for not measuring the HR department overall. First, some feel that since evaluation has not been demanded in the past, why offer it now? OD staffs have chosen not to pick up the signals from line managers who reluctantly settle for subjective assessments of the outcomes. Since management has not pressed the issue most OD staffs are content to let it lie.

A second reason why it does not happen is a combination of fear and responsibility. Mirvis and Berg,[4] in their book on failures in OD, point out that the necessity to carry out successful change programs and thereby acquire budgets to do more work has created conditions tempting, if not causing, practitioners to devalue unpleasant information, to destroy unsavory findings, and to deny responsibility when their efforts fail. I have personally experienced that with OD people. The most flagrant example was a well-known consultant who disavowed any responsibility for a suicide which took place after one of his encounter sessions. The fact that he led a person through an exercise which touched off such an act of violence and that he did not have the ability to deal with it did not seem to concern him. The fear of failure, and more importantly the fear of having to accept responsibility for a major part of the failure, is enough to keep many practitioners away from OD evaluation.

The next pretext has to do with ignorance. Many OD staffs simply do not know how to measure. The U.S. Department of Health, Education, and Welfare studied 34 cases of work experiments which claimed unqualified improvements. A host of critics have challenged the results, pointing out that invalid and unreliable documentation was presented. Assuming that the reporters were not deliberately trying to deceive, we can only conclude that their knowledge of measurement methods was extremely weak. In their defense, it should be noted that opportunities for gaining knowledge and skill in field experimentation is very limited in industry. That is not a justification; it is just a small problem to be surmounted.

The last and most difficult obstacle to overcome is that many practitioners do not want to measure. The idea of measurement, proof, or the very introduction of objective methods into the field goes against the value system of a large segment of the OD profession. They believe that OD should be excused from the rigors of scientific method. The position is that this somehow impedes the process, focuses the effort on irrelevant matters, and makes the whole thing less useful or usable. Some people who hold this position are close to being fanatic about it. Some are zealous in their love for OD, and a few are almost manic about its special purpose and value. These people love the process of OD so much that they cannot accept the constraints that science imposes. The irony is that although they sometimes deal with the most intimate issues in the lives of their clients, they do not want to stop to look at the effects of their work. These types of persons will probably never be persuaded to measure their outcomes.

The job of the HR department manager is to convince the OD staff that there is a necessity for some type of objective evaluation of their work. Personnel has reached a point in recent years where it no longer asks the business world to accept it purely for its inherent "goodness." OD has yet to reach that point. The following discussion hopefully will provide both sides with enough measurement alternatives that a few suitable ones can be adopted.

MEASURES OF EFFECTIVENESS FOR ORGANIZATION DEVELOPMENT

The objective of the remainder of this chapter will be to demonstrate how the effectiveness of both individuals and the organization can be evaluated at points across three levels. You will see how you can start with several broadly stated criterion variables and find measurement opportunities with subsystems and with specific independent variables.

Before any OD project gets underway the first question must be, "why are we doing this project?" Another way of stating it is, "what is the problem?" A penetrating and truthful answer to this type of question will point out the issue which may be measurable. If that is too simple or does not yield a satisfactory answer, the framework which follows should reveal it.

The five criterion variables in Fig. 15.1 have a time aspect to them. The time dimension enters the picture when an organization is conceptualized as an element of a larger system (the environment). The organization, over time, takes, processes, and returns resources to the environment. Accordingly, a time line with three ranges can be constructed. These ranges describe broad periods in an organization's life cycle. They are the *short run, intermediate,* and *long run.* Some of the criteria exist across all time periods while others are primarily period-oriented.

The Xs indicate the time period of primary consideration. Clearly, issues such as production are always important. Nevertheless, the focus is usually on the short term. Each criterion has goals and objectives which can be defined, described, and measured.

CRITERIA

1. Production. Production reflects the basic ability of the organization to produce the goods and services in the quantity and quality which the market demands. Examples of production criteria are tons of steel, barrels of beer, dollars of sales, invoices processed, and new accounts opened. These are the dependent variables (outcomes) which are affected by an OD intervention, e.g., team building, work flow redesign, and conflict resolution.

The typical question asked is, "I don't see how I can relate a small OD effort to the number of tons of steel my mill rolled last month." The answer is, "You can't." Redesigning the work flow of the quality control department will probably not affect the number of tons of steel rolled, but it may affect the efficiency of the quality control department. If it improves the throughput of inspections or tests, that is a cost savings which does affect the organization's profitability. Keep the measure connected to the appropriate variable. If you want to impact tonnage

	Time period		
	Short run	Intermediate	Long run
Criterion variables:			
Production	X		
Efficiency	X		
Satisfaction	X		
Adaptiveness		X	
Development		X	
Survival			X

Figure 15.1 Criterion Variables for Organizational Development

output, go to the places in the mill where that takes place. Look for opportunities for OD techniques to solve production-related problems. There are many people-based activities in a rolling mill that OD might be able to improve.

2. Efficiency.   This is generally defined as the ratio of outputs to inputs. Measures of efficiency include rate of return on assets, unit cost, scrap and waste, machine downtime, cost per hire, and time to process an invoice.

A team-building project which produces an improved invoice processing time may not be as exciting as one which changes a supervisor's leadership style, but it is a lot easier to measure. It probably also has a much better chance of happening. A change of style may improve the efficiency or effectiveness of a work group. If it does, you should be able to establish that fact and quantify the benefit which ensued.

3. Satisfaction.   Since an organization is in part a social system, we are concerned with employee feelings. They are important because people are intrinsically important. Feelings are also important because they impact individual productivity. OD people like to spend time dealing with the emotional side of the enterprise. They could measure the outcomes of their work in several ways. Issues which have a large emotional component are turnover, absence, tardiness, and grievances. OD work could show a correlation with changes in any of these phenomena.

It is clear from the material we have presented so far that OD can do many things of value besides making people feel good. Positive attitudes, reduced stress, strong group cohesiveness, and supportive interpersonal relationships can all be related to organizational productivity or effectiveness variables. When you look into subsystems, you will find specific examples of those types of variables.

4. Adaptiveness.   As we move from the short run to intermediate outcomes, it becomes more difficult but not impossible to find measures. In the case of adaptiveness, the only true test is when the company is faced with a need or opportunity and it rises to or fails to meet the test. OD probably can do a lot in this arena, but it would be difficult to show cause and effect relationships. The reason for the difficulty is the intervening time. You may conduct a series of very useful team-building sessions and a year later the company is able to shift strategies much faster than they used to. You know that your work had a lot to do with that improved capability but you can only infer, not prove, it.

5. Development.   An organization must invest in itself in order to enhance its capability for survival. The measures here are not training programs or interventions run, but rather knowledge and skills attained and used to achieve positive results. Much of industry training is really education, as we pointed out in the previous chapter. It deals with concepts and increases the learner's breadth of knowledge. Knowledge is useful in helping people be more aware and logical, and it can give them more information with which they can improve their decision-making abilities. However, skills also have to be developed. OD teaches people skills through simulations or on-the-job training. It helps people learn how to increase their ability to interact, supervise, and be supervised. The types of development activities which are easiest to measure are the ones carried out in formal classroom settings (described in Chapter 14). OD can do some of the same type of measurement if it carefully selects some baseline data before beginning its intervention. The OD consultant has a great deal of control over the intervention environment. Most interactive change efforts are less structured than a classroom training session. Nevertheless, they are, or should be, directed toward some goal. Either the goal or a subset of the goal will be visible behavior or concrete organizational results, which are usually quantifiable.

6. Survival.   Only in rare cases is an OD intervention close enough to a survival crisis for a cause and effect relationship to be drawn. There is enough work for OD to do with the preceding criteria that it can pass on this one.

SUBSYSTEMS

Within each of the criteria above we can find subsystems operating. A subsystem has three phases: input, process, and output (I-P-O). As we shift from the broad criteria, through the subsystems, to the individual variables, we find an increasing number of opportunities to measure. Keep in mind that the intervention and the measure have to be related to each other. This relationship must be established at the beginning for maximum credibility.

1. Production.   The inputs to the production process are

- People
- Machines   All working together
- Material   on intermediate or final
- Energy   processes to create outputs
- Capital

OD is involved with the way that the inputs, principally people, interact during the process stage. Examples of processes and their outputs are

- Brewing an output which is beer
- Digging an output which is ore
- Assembling an output which is circuit boards
- Forming/shaping an output which is metal/plastic/wood components
- Installing an output which is telephones
- Cashing checks an output which is money
- Screening applicants an output which is candidates

Some of the above are the end product of a company while some are both the end product of a department and an intermediate product of the company. Since OD might be involved with people as they carry out any of the above processes, it can be shown how the OD intervention impacts the cost, process time, quality, or quantity of the outputs. This leads us to the next subsystem.

2. Efficiency.   This is the arena in which the measurement is actually taken. It answers how well the I-P-O subsystem is operating. The variables in the situation have values attached to them and ratios calculated for them. The formulas are self-evident. You add all the inputs and divide the output by them for a measure of productivity. If you want to look at the picture from the other side, you can reverse the ratio and divide the inputs by the output and find the resource requirement. The inverse is particularly helpful for very complex situations.

An OD project may deal with the behavior of the input variable, people, as they interact in the process and be able to demonstrate that the group's output goals were met or exceeded. Surveys and interviews may also uncover data on other inputs which, if acted on, could improve ratios. OD has many faces and many tools. Measurement is possible in many different combinations.

3. Satisfaction.   This subsystem deals principally with the realm of feelings and attitudes. The inputs are not only people but the things in the workplace which impinge on the people and to which they must react. The I-P-O model is shown in Fig. 15.2.

Clearly, the outputs are measurable. The satisfaction arena is a favorite one of the OD staff. They are committed to making the work place a more humanistic environment. If they can connect the human-

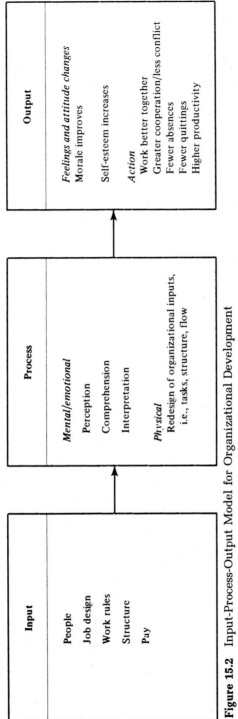

Figure 15.2 Input-Process-Output Model for Organizational Development

istic issues to improved feelings and attitudes and relate that to improvements in work variables, they can easily show the value of their work in business terms.

Adaptability and development utilize the same I-P-O model, but they experience it over a longer time frame. The task for the OD practitioner is to be able to connect the work being done today on the criterion variables of efficiency and satisfaction with the intermediate criteria of adaptability and development. This is difficult to prove at the .05 level of significance. However, sometimes a valid, easy to accept inference can be established.

VARIABLES

Each phase in the I-P-O model has a number of variables which interact to contribute to the health and effectiveness of the individual and the organization. Many of these are quantifiable.

Phase	Productivity/effectiveness	Health
Inputs Programmers Salaries Computers Job descriptions	Baseline data gathered before intervention on costs, timeliness, quantity and quality of work, as well as the attitudes and feelings (and maybe interpersonal skills) of the programmers.	
Processes Writing code and documenting program Writing user manuals Communications	Systematic observations and data collection which lead the organizational development consultant to design the intervention which seems most appropriate.	
Outputs Programs	Reliability, efficiency, cost, on-time completion, amount of redesign	Fatigue and stress levels
User reactions	Satisfaction with design and capability acceptance without revision	
Documentation	Readability, completeness	
Manuals	Trainees' and operators' acceptance or complaints	
Feelings and inter-personal behavior		Degree of satisfaction, stimulation, clarity about job, cooperation, accomplishment

Figure 15.3   Variables Affected by Organizational Development Intervention

Assume that an OD intervention was held within a computer programming department. It could be that there had been conflict, unclear expectations, or other interpersonal issues which were affecting the output of the department. In Fig. 15.3 you will find a number of variables which could be quantified on a before and after basis to measure the change which resulted from the intervention. Two types of changes are measurable. One relates to health and the other relates to productivity and effectiveness.

The variable list is obviously not all-inclusive. I am sure you can think of many more items which could be evaluated. The key seems to be the evaluator's ability to dissect an input, a process, or an output into the many subvariables or elements which constitute it. If you will take the time up front to understand the environment, just as you do when constructing the matrix, you will have no trouble finding variables to measure.

ORGANIZATION DEVELOPMENT AND PRODUCTIVITY

In a research project carried out with over 1500 workers between 1978 and 1982 we looked at 150 variables which might impact an employee's productivity.[5] Early on we used factor analysis to arrange them into 22 factors or clusters (see Fig. 15.4). Later, we regressed the factors against a productivity criterion and uncovered those factors which affected each work group's productivity.

OD can work on the belief system and the feelings of workers toward all of these factors. It can demonstrate change for the better on any of them. That in itself would be a significant achievement. Using our program, the OD consultant can extract the factors which impact productivity in a given work group. Then the consultant can carry out the OD intervention and show management how it has positively affected the group's productivity.

I firmly believe, based on better than 15 years of contact with organizational development, that the issue of measurability is overwhelmingly one of misguided and conflicting values. If you can show your OD staff how they can serve both the worker and the organization by focusing on desirable outcomes, and that measuring those outcomes will prove to be a positive experience, you might be able to overcome the value bias. OD is a methodology of great promise, but it needs to realize that it is operating in an organization and therefore must serve the needs of the organization as well as those of the worker. The needs of the organization are quantifiable. It is not a sellout to quantitatively evaluate the good which comes from an OD intervention. Unless OD shifts its beliefs about measurement and responsibility for results, it will never live up to the power it has to change organizational life for the better.

---

1. **Leader behavior**—Supervisor's way of dealing with people, work flow, and resource issues.

2. **Worker behavior**—Work-related interactions with coworkers and supervisor.

3. **Delegation**—Amount and manner in which supervisor delegates and encourages new ideas.

4. **Worker capability**—Skill, knowledge, experience, education, and potential which the worker brings to the job.

5. **Strictness**—Firm and equitable enforcement of the company rules and procedures.

6. **Equipment design**—Degree of difficulty experienced in operating equipment.

7. **Job satisfaction**—Worker's general attitude and satisfaction with the job.

8. **External influences**—Effects of outside social, political, and economic activity.

9. **Safety**—Company's efforts to provide a safe and healthy working environment.

10. **Self-responsibility**—Workers' concern for quality and their desire to be responsible.

11. **Resources**—Availability of tools, manuals, parts, and material needed to do the job.

12. **Country's situation**—Impact of national conditions on the worker and the company.

13. **Coworkers**—Mutual respect and liking among the members of the work group.

14. **Pay and conditions of work**—Performance reviews, promotions, pay, and work scheduling.

15. **Job stress**—Environmental effects, such as temperature and ventilation, plus feelings about job security.

16. **Personal problems**—Impact of overtime on personal life, and other personal life issues.

17. **Self-esteem**—Sense of self-respect and respect from others derived from doing the job.

18. **Work problems**—Physical and psychological fatigue resulting from work.

19. **The company**—General attitudes toward the company, its style of operation, and its stability.

20. **Economic needs**—Degree to which the job satisfies workers' needs for food, clothing, and shelter.

21. **Responsibility accepted**—Desired workload and responsibility versus actual workload and responsibility.

22. **Company policies**—Rest periods, training, job layout, and departmental characteristics.

---

*This list does not imply there will always be 22 factors. Each set of data will cluster according to its particular nature. The chances are more likely that the number of factors will decrease slightly rather than increase.

Figure 15.4 Productivity Factors*

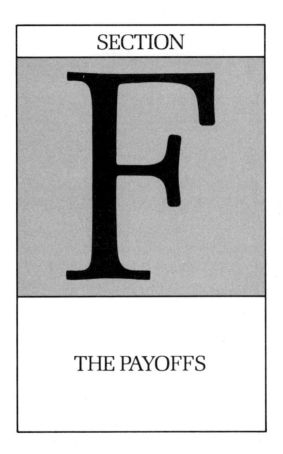

SECTION

F

THE PAYOFFS

CHAPTER

16

Principles of Performance Measurement

In the early chapters I stated that there are many payoffs to be derived from an HR department measurement system. They are available at all levels from the individual to the organizational. Hopefully, you have seen many of them as you have studied the formulas and figures. I want to conclude the book by reviewing the basic principles of objective performance measurement and by discussing briefly the individual and organizational payoffs which a measurement system can generate.

There are five points about measurement which I believe are underlying principles. I have covered them all throughout the book, but they bear repeating.

1. The productivity and effectiveness of any function can be measured by some combination of cost, time, quantity, or quality indices. Some functions lend themselves to objective evaluation better than others. However, I have yet to find one which does not allow for any quantitative appraisal. Critics will come up with all sorts of reasons why something cannot or should not be measured. Nevertheless, you can find something meaningful to measure if you remember to look for observable, describable phenomena in the process. Even such seemingly esoteric work as research and development yields opportunities for objective assessment of activities and results. In the early 1970s Hughes Aircraft conducted an extensive study of productivity within R & D.[1] A perusal of the study report uncovers dozens of quantitative issues suitable for measurement.

213

2. A measurement system promotes productivity by for ¬ing attention on the important issues, tasks, and objectives.   Over the 20 plus years I have worked in organizations the single most counterproductivè factor I have observed is lack of clarity about priorities. The causes would probably take a book to explain. However, I am more interested in finding remedies rather than lamenting over the reasons why it goes on. My experience with measurement systems is that they help to clarify what is to be accomplished and how well it should be done. I believe that if you can get these two points across to people you have carried out two of the three most critical tasks of management. The third is providing support in the form of information, supplies, tools, and humanistic treatment. The value of the systems approach is that it takes into consideration the total mission of the department. In doing that it leaves nothing to chance and little room for misperception of priorities. I have great faith in people. I know that if management gives workers what they need, the people will find a way to meet the objectives of the organization.

3. Professional and knowledge workers are best measured as a group.
Professional people do not like to think of themselves as automatons. And they aren't. Their work requires thought, independent judgment and action, and interpersonal cooperation. In order to be optimally effective a professional group has to work together. If you try to measure the work of each person individually and compare them against their colleagues, you are asking for trouble. Comparison leads to competition rather than cooperation. It breaks down cohesiveness because the objective shifts from group to individual performance. It's an issue of survival: when you try to measure individually people are smart enough to know how to protect themselves. Threat forces defensiveness, and defensiveness leads to data manipulation. If that occurs, you are sunk. I don't have to explain what bad data will do to you. On the other hand, when you build a system based on group objectives you do not have to worry about laggards. Peer pressure will stimulate the low performer, and if that doesn't work you will certainly be told by someone in the group that there is a problem. I once worked for a very wise man who operated under the motto, "if we succeed there is glory enough for everyone; but, if we fail there are no heroes."

4. Managers can be measured by the efficiency and effectiveness of the units they manage.   It is true that a good group can overcome an inept manager. However, before long it will be clear that there is a managerial void. If the nature of managerial work is to get things done through other people, then it must follow that a manager's performance is reflected in the output of the group. Managers do many things, and they can be observed and objectively evaluated. However, that would miss the mark. I have known managers who were picture perfect on the surface, but when you put them in charge they can't get results. This is one of the vexing problems with assessment centers. Some people look great in a simulation. They know the theory and they know how to play the game. But, they can't manage a two-car parade.

5. The ultimate measurement is not efficiency, but effectiveness. The highest form of organizational excellence is to create the greatest good with the least input. That is more than being efficient. It implies being maximally efficient and productive with materials and people. In addition, it requires that the resources be directed toward the objectives which are most prized. That means focusing on results, doing the right thing at the right time, and serving long-term as well as short-term goals. In order for an organization to achieve optimum effectiveness it needs a sound operating philosophy which is communicated to all employees, good planning toward worthwhile objectives, and a monitoring system which tells it whether or not it is moving toward those objectives in an acceptable fashion. The measurement system plays a crucial part in the last step.

The five points above are the principles around which a measurement system should be constructed. I can tell you from years of trial and error that if you violate them they will burn you sooner or later. But if you use them as the framework of your system the payoffs will be many and long-lasting.

Organizational Payoffs

The human resources function permeates the whole organization. Whether it is acknowledged or not, the HR department makes a significant positive or negative impact on its organization. Cascio[2] gives examples of a half-dozen areas where the effectiveness of the HR department impacts the bottom line.

COMPENSATION

Organizations which neglect their pay system inevitably either overpay or underpay their employees. The outcome is that the overpaid incompetents stay and the underpaid competent employees leave. Not only does the organization end up paying too much for what they have; they incur unnecessary turnover expenses.

BENEFITS

An attentive benefits manager makes sure that any dividends or refunds which are due the organization from the carrier are paid promptly. A dollar received is a dollar which does not have to be borrowed at double-digit interest rates. Tardiness and absence have to be monitored or an organization pays for people not to work. I was in a company once which did not keep track of absences of professionals and managers. Since no one seemed to care, the people got the signal that absence of any amount was acceptable. The effects of absence were shown in Chapter 12.

PERSONNEL TAXES

Turnover management shows its effect in this area as well as others. Since unemployment insurance taxes are usually based on work force turnover experience, high turnover takes money directly out of the corporate profits. Payroll unemployment insurance taxes run from 1.5 to about 4 percent of payroll for most companies. An effective claims management program can keep the firm's contribution toward the lower end. When I came into one company the tax rate was almost 4 percent. Over a period of 3 years we were able to lower it to less than 2 percent, which was a savings of $1 million on the company's $50 million payroll. Social security taxes are also swollen by turnover. If you have to make contributions to the maximum for two or three highly paid employees in the same job in 1 year, costs can double.

STAFFING

It is a sad fact that many people hold jobs for which they are over-qualified. This results in an employee who is not highly motivated, is overpaid, and is a candidate for turnover. Good recruiters learn what is really needed in the departments which they service. They persuade managers to cast the job at the right level and pay the appropriate salary. This keeps down salary expense and curbs turnover expense. Another aspect of the employment program is selection. Several years ago people got scared out of testing for selection for fear of discrimination claims. Now, selection testing is more sophisticated. It does a better job of screening out people who have little chance of succeeding. A good selection system cuts down turnover. In the 1960s a firm I worked with was losing nearly 50 percent of their newly hired MBAs within the first year. Once we got them to pay more attention to their selection and training system the losses dropped to 10 percent. Considering that first-year costs for salaries and training were running about $20,000, this change in the program saved the company over $300,000.

AFFIRMATIVE ACTION

EEO is more than avoiding lawsuits. There are many highly motivated, loyal, qualified minorities and women inside companies who could receive further training and promotions. Under pressure to redress the inequities of the past, many organizations are hiring young, inexperienced minorities and women just to meet goals, and often these young people really are not equipped for higher-level jobs. They should be hired at the entry level and the current minority and female populations should be trained for the higher-level jobs. It would save money and avoid a host of other problems as well. Obviously, saving the organization from discrimination and unfair labor practice suits has a financial benefit.

TURNOVER

Some turnover is inevitable. Layoffs are sometimes unavoidable. Judicious use of outplacement services can cut severance expense and make the outgoing employee much happier. Exit interview programs can help ferret out the source of a turnover problem. Prompt counseling can turn a questionable firing or a productivity-robbing morale problem into a mutually agreeable resolution. The solution may even be a voluntary quit, which would be better than a lawsuit with all its attendant costs.

SUMMARY

These are a few of the many ways that the HR department works to reduce organizational expenses and inversely helps increase profits. Measurement contributes to this in several ways:

- Alerts management to problems early
- Identifies opportunities for greater efficiencies
- By showing positive results it stimulates people to do even better

Individual Payoffs

The only reason that people do anything is because they see some kind of payoff for their effort. This does not mean that they are selfish, self-centered, or greedy. It is simply normal behavior. People do not act randomly, that is, they must have a reason for doing something. That reason may be to avoid pain or it may be to experience pleasure. It may also be just to maintain the status quo which is a little bit of each of the above. Only people who are suffering from some type of mental or emotional disorder act in ways which are detrimental to themselves. Granted, it is true that we all do things which do ourselves harm. But they are not intended to end up like that. We expect that we are doing what is right for us, but once in a while we make a mistake. All this is by way of saying that if you want your staff to get behind a measurement system you need to show them what the payoffs will be.

If you ask employees of any personnel department how good a job they are doing, the chances are high that they will reply positively. Then if you ask them to prove it they probably won't be able to. So here is the first payoff. Numbers can be proof, whereas words are just sounds. For the first time, the people will be able to prove that they are doing an excellent job. No one will be able to deny them. They will be able to show month after month that either they are improving or they are maintaining a high level of proficiency.

Another very important reward that stems from that is self-satisfaction. Without a measurement system all they are sure of is that they are working like the devil, processing a lot of people or paper, and aren't seeing any end in sight. They have no sense of accomplishment because they don't know what they have done. All they can be sure of is that they put in a lot of effort and probably got very little recognition for it. This reward is a very personal one.

The productivity research project described in the previous chapter has proven that self-esteem and self-respect, as it relates to the job, are prerequisites to high productivity. One of the major problems personnel people have always had is low self-esteem. One reason why is that they could never show they were making a contribution to the bottom line.

A third payoff is power. The people will be able to come to you and prove that they need more resources. You will be able to take that proof to management and get it for them. It is the third level of success that was described in the beginning of this chapter. There won't be any need to beg, threaten, or argue. The numbers will speak for themselves. At long last, your department will get the people, equipment, space, or money that it deserves.

Finally, the development and use of your measurement system will provide the people with the organizational rewards they deserve. You will be able to demonstrate that their jobs and salaries should be leveled according to their contributions—contributions which can be substantiated. You will be able to obtain salary increases for them which truly reflect not just their effort but their accomplishments. The money, titles, and status which they have been denied in the past will now come. They will have to come because they cannot be denied. The days of second-class citizenship will be over. Your people can stop going around like Rodney Dangerfield complaining that they "don't get no respect around here." They will get it because they will prove that they have earned it.

Conclusion:
Success Revisited

In Section A I talked about the abilities required for a person to be successful in an organization. The first is the ability to excel at your job. You are already doing that. Second is the ability to select the issues which are important to the larger organization and to direct your efforts toward them. I hope you are doing that. Third is the ability to develop performance data from your work and to use it to inform and persuade. Throughout the book I have focused on this last ability. The objective has been to help you develop the skill to extract objective data from the results of your work and to put it in forms which will influence the thinking of your various audiences. It is naive to believe that in an organization which may employ anywhere from a few hundred to many thousands of people all you have to do is keep your nose to the grindstone and you will succeed. Organizations are finite institutions. They do not have unlimited resources, and there are many contenders for those resources. In order to get your rightful share you must be able to demonstrate that there is a good business reason for giving it to you.

Although human resources work may have some intrinsic goodness about it in terms of helping people learn, grow, and advance, organizations do not tend to pay much for goodness. They are, out of necessity, most interested in return on investment. Once you can prove that something you did made a contribution to that magic bottom line you get what you need to continue to excel at your job. Beyond that, you will get the respect that you deserve as a professional and as a member of the management team.

The founder of a major semiconductor company told me, "When I was young I thought it was enough just to be right. After I got fired for being right, I realized that you have to be right and have power."

Numbers are power. Good luck.

References

SECTION A

1. G. S. Odiorne, *Management by Objectives Newsletter,* July 1974.
2. P. Drucker, *Management: Tasks, Responsibilities and Practices,* Harper and Row, New York, 1973, p. 45.
3. John Donne, *Devotions XVII.*
4. H. C. White and M. N. Wolfe, "The Role Desired for Personnel Administration," Arizona University, Department of Management, Tempe, AZ, January 1980.
5. ———, "Human Resources Management in U.S. Industry: Current Status and Future Directions," Opinion Research Corporation, Princeton, NJ, December 1979.
6. T. F. Cawsey, "Why Line Managers Don't Listen to Their Personnel Departments," *Personnel,* January–February 1980, p. 14.

SECTION B

1. J. L. Grahn, "White Collar Productivity: Misunderstandings and Some Progress," *Personnel Administration,* August 1981, p. 30.
2. H. Dahl and K. S. Morgan, "Return on Investment in Human Resources," in R. N. Lehrer, ed., *White Collar Productivity,* McGraw-Hill, New York, 1983, p. 282.
3. E. H. Burack and N. J. Mathys, *Human Resource Planning: A Pragmatic Approach to Manpower Staffing and Development,* Brace-Park Press, Lake Forest, IL, 1980, p. 121.

SECTION C

1. Edward E. Lawler III, *Pay and Organizational Effectiveness: A Psychological View,* McGraw-Hill, New York, 1971, p. 59.
2. Henry C. Smith and John H. Wakeley, *Psychology of Industrial Behavior,* 3d ed., McGraw-Hill, New York, 1972, pp. 243–244.

SECTION D

1. T. Gallwey, *The Inner Game of Tennis,* Random House, New York, 1974.
2. M. Fishbein and I. Ajzen, *Belief, Attitude, Intention and Behavior: An Introduction to Theory and Research,* Addison-Wesley, Reading, MA, 1975, Preface, p. v.
3. F. E. Kuzmits, "How Much is Absenteeism Costing Your Organization?," *Personnel Administrator,* June 1979.
4. J. L. Price, *The Study of Turnover,* Iowa State Press, Ames, IA, 1977.
5. T. Hall, "How to Estimate Employee Turnover Cost," *Personnel,* July–August 1981, pp. 43–52.

SECTION E

1. R. F. Mager, *Preparing Instructional Objectives,* Fearon Publishers, Inc., Belmont, CA, 1975, Preface.
2. E. H. Schein, *Organizational Psychology,* Prentice-Hall, Inc., Englewood Cliffs, NJ, 1965, p. 8.
3. R. Beckhard, *Organization Development: Strategies and Models,* Addison-Wesley, Reading, MA, 1969, p. 9.
4. P. H. Mirvis and David N. Berg, *Failures in Organization Development and Change,* John Wiley & Sons, Inc., New York, 1977.
5. J. Fitz-enz, "What Causes People to be Productive," Saratoga Institute, Saratoga, CA, 1982.

SECTION F

1. J. Fitz-enz, *R & D Productivity,* Hughes Aircraft Co., Culver City, CA, 1978.
2. W. F. Cascio, *Costing Human Resources: The Financial Impact of Behavior in Organizations,* Kent Publishing Co., Boston, MA, 1982, pp. 8–12.

Bibliography

Balk, W. L., "Technological Trends in Productivity Management," *Public Personnel Management,* March–April, 1975, pp. 128–133.

Blakeney, R. N., M. T. Matteson, and J. Huff, "The Personnel Function: A Systemic View," *Public Personnel Management,* January–February 1974, pp. 83–86.

Bolar, M., "Measuring Effectiveness of Personnel Policy Implementation," *Personnel Psychology,* 1970, pp. 463–480.

Boylen, M. E., "The Four Costs of Employee Training," *Administrative Management,* March, 1980, pp. 40–41.

Brack, G. E., "Allocating Personnel Department Costs," *Management Accounting,* May, 1975, pp. 48–50.

Burton, R. and A. S. Tsui, "Human Resource Management in Complex Organizations," Paper presented at the National Meeting of the Institute for Management Sciences, San Diego, 1982.

Carr, C. B. Jr., "Total Turnover," *Personnel Journal,* July 1972, pp. 524–527.

Carroll, S. J. Jr., "Measuring The Work of a Personnel Department," *Personnel,* 1960, pp. 49–56.

Cawsey, T. F., "Why Line Managers Don't Listen to Their Personnel Departments," *Personnel,* AMACOM, American Management Association, pp. 11–20.

——— and W. C. Wedley, "Labor Turnover Costs: Measurement and Control," *Personnel Journal,* February 1979, pp. 90–95.

Clarke, E., "Improving White Collar Productivity," *Electronic Engineering Times,* September 29, 1980, pp. 89–90.

Connolly, T., E. Conlon, and Deutsch, "A Multiple Constituency Approach of Organizational Effectiveness," *Academy of Management Review,* 1980, pp. 211–218.

Dahl, H. and K. S. Morgan, "Is Anyone Measuring Return on Investment in Human Resources?," *Upjohn Company Report,* 1981.

———, "Return on Investment in Human Resources," *Upjohn Company Report,* 1982.

Driessnack, C. H., "Financial Impact of Effective Human Resources Management," *The Personnel Administrator,* December 1979, pp. 62–66.

"Education in Industry—Today and in the Future," *Training and Development Journal,* May 1976, pp. 30–34.

"Employment Cost Index," *Current Wage Developments,* September 1980, pp. 40–42.

Fitz-enz, J., "Quantifying the Human Resources Function," *Personnel,* AMACOM, American Management Association, 1980.

———, "The Measurement Imperative," *Personnel Journal,* April 1978, pp. 193–195.

———, "Measuring Human Resources Effectiveness," *Personnel Administrator,* July 1980, pp. 33–36.

———, Kathryn Hards, and G. E. Savage, "Total Development: Selection, Assessment, Growth," *Personnel Administrator,* February 1980, pp. 58–62.

——— and K. Hards, "How to Make Sure Your Department Survives the Next Recession," *Training/HRD,* August 1978, pp. 88–92.

Gordon, M. E., "Three Ways to Effectively Evaluate Personnel Programs," *Personnel Journal,* July 1972, pp. 498–504.

Hartman, R. I., and J. J. Gibson, "The Persistent Problem of Employee Absenteeism," *Personnel Journal,* July 1971, pp. 535–539.

Heda, S. S., and M. B. Shirk, "Human Resources Accounting System and Productivity Monitoring," *Hospital & Health Services Administration,* Fall 1979, pp. 36–45.

Hedges, J. N., "Absence from Work—Measuring the Hours Lost," *Monthly Labor Review,* October 1977, pp. 16–23.

———, "Employee Absenteeism and Turnover," The Bureau of National Affairs, Washington, D. C., May 1974.

Horrigan, J. T., "The Effects of Training on Turnover: A Cost Justification Model," *Training and Development Journal,* July 1979, pp. 3–7.

"Is Personnel Still Underpowered?," *Personnel Management,* June 1973, pp. 34–35.

Kearsley, G., and T. Compton, "Assessing Costs, Benefits and Productivity in Training Systems," *Training and Development Journal,* January 1981, pp. 52–58.

Kuzmits, F. E., "How Much Is Absenteeism Costing Your Organization?" *The Personnel Administrator,* June 1979, pp. 29–33.

Lawrence, D. B., "Consensus: Personnel Ratios: 1978 Food-For-Thought Figures," *Personnel,* January–February 1979, pp. 4–10.

Lawson, J. W. II, and B. F. Smith, "Cost of Benefits," *Management's Complete Guide to Employee Benefits,* Dartnell, Chicago, 1980, Chapter 3.

Lowman, J., and T. Snediker, "Pinpointing Avoidable Turnover with 'Cohort Analysis,'" *Personnel Journal,* April 1980, pp. 310–312.

Luthans, F., and T. L. Maris, "Evaluating Personnel Programs Through the Reversal Technique," *Personnel Journal,* October 1979, pp. 692–697.

McAfee, R. B., "Evaluating the Personnel Department's Internal Functioning," *Personnel,* May–June 1980, pp. 56–62.

McCarthy, J. P., "Memo to Senior Management: Is Your Personnel Department Effective?," *Best's Review,* July 1980, pp. 101–105.

McLaughlin, D., "Roadblocks to Personnel Department Effectiveness," *Personnel Journal,* 1971, pp. 56–62.

Malone, R. L., and D. J. Petersen, "Personnel Effectiveness: Its Dimensions and Development," *Personnel Journal,* October 1977, pp. 498–501.

———, "The Personnel Effectiveness Grid (PEG): A New Tool for Estimating Personnel Department Effectiveness," *Human Resource Management,* Winter 1975, pp. 10–21.

Miner, M. G., "Job Absence and Turnover: A New Source of Data," *Monthly Labor Review,* October 1977, pp. 24–31.

———, "Personnel Budgets and Staffs: How Big Should They Be?," *Personnel Administrator,* July 1980, pp. 51–55.

Mirvis, P. H., and E. E. Lawler, "Measuring the Financial Impact of Employee Attitudes," *Journal of Applied Psychology,* 1977, vol. 62, no. 1, pp. 9–15.

Odiorne, G. S., "The Need For an Economic Approach to Training," *Training and Development Journal,* June 1979, pp. 32–40.

"Organizing and Staffing the Personnel Function: Guidelines for Evaluation," *Harvard Business Review,* May–June 1977.

"Personnel and Productivity," *Management Today,* July 1979.

Phillips, J. J., *Handbook of Training Evaluation and Measurement Methods,* Gulf Publishing Co., Houston, TX, 1983.

Rabe, W. F., "Yardsticks for Measuring Personnel Department Effectiveness," *Personnel,* January–February 1967, pp. 56–62.

Raisin, J., "Researching Our Own Effectiveness," *Personnel Management,* 1981, p. 3.

Rand, J. F., "Accountability Management and Productivity Bargaining," *Personnel Journal,* March 1978, pp. 154–158.

"Reducing Labor Turnover Costs," *The CPA,* November 1975, pp. 75–77.

Stone, T. H., "Absence Control: Is Your Company a Candidate?" *Personnel Administrator,* September 1980, pp. 77–82.

"To Survive the Budget Inquisition, Prove Your Training Makes Dollars and Sense," *Training/HRD,* November 1980, pp. 23–25.

Szilagyi, A. D., "Keeping Employee Turnover Under Control," *Personnel,* November–December 1979, pp. 42–52.

Udler, A. S., "Productivity Measurement of Administrative Services," *Personnel Journal,* December 1978, pp. 672–697.

—— and J. D. Cole, "Productivity and Personnel," *Civil Service Journal,* October–December 1976, pp. 23–27.

Wage and Salary Administration, The Bureau of National Affairs, Washington, D. C., July 1972.

Zippo, M., "Personnel Activities: Where the Dollars Went in 1979," *Personnel,* January 1980, pp. 65–66.

Index

ABOUT THE AUTHOR

Dr. Jac Fitz-enz is currently president of Saratoga Institute, a human resources research and consulting company, headquartered in Saratoga, California. Previously he held the positions of vice-president for industrial relations at Four-Phase Systems, vice-president of organization development for Imperial Bank, and manager of personnel and training at Wells Fargo Bank. Since 1978 he has conducted workshops on human resources management nationwide, and he has published numerous articles in professional journals.